Brown Eyes, Blue Eyes:
Linking Perceptions and Performance
Facilitator Guide

Indra Lahiri, Ph.D.

BULLSEYE PUBLISHING

1

Brown Eyes, Blue Eyes:
Linking Perceptions and Performance
Facilitator Guide

For information, contact:

Bullseye Publishing
750 Allentown Rd
Sellersville, PA 18960 USA
www.workforcedevelopmentgroup.com
(215) 453-8577

Book and cover design by Kimberlee Jensen, IsisEye Media.

Book production by Workforce Development Group.

Printed in the United States of America.

Library of Congress Cataloguing-in-Publication Data

Lahiri, Indra
    Brown Eyes, Blue Eyes Facilitator Guide: Linking Perceptions and Performance/ Indra Lahiri, PhD.

    ISBN 0-9721758-0-6
    1.   Diversity education–Prejudice–Discrimination–Eye of the Storm–A Class Divided–Angry Eye–Essential Blue-eyed–Handbooks, manuals, etc. Lahiri, Indra 1969-. Title.

Brown Eyes, Blue Eyes:
Linking Perceptions and Performance
Facilitator Guide

Acknowledgments

Grateful acknowledgment is made to all those who made this book possible, just a few of whom are named here:

Jane Elliott, for her fearless, tireless, and ingenious work in combatting all forms of prejudice, and for her generous help and feedback on this document.

Sheila Haji, for inspiration, friendship, wisdom, mentoring, and invaluable input on the content of this guide. Without Sheila, none of this work would have been possible.

Debbie Danuser, Sheri Leppink and MaryJo Scarpelli from Trainer's Toolchest, for their enthusiasm, counsel, and being an overall joy to work with.

Admire Entertainment, PBS Video, California Newsreel, and Guidance Associates for their cooperation and support.

Debbie Welker and Joanne Cunningham for believing and keeping me motivated, being all-around wonderful, plus for a whole lot of editing and proofreading.

Countless participants in workshops that I have facilitated, who taught me how to design a workshop, and how to help others learn.

My parents, who taught me there is no such thing as "I can't".

Dr. Austin Sedicum, my chief editor, partner, best friend, and source of endless joy.

Facilitator Guide

Brown Eyes, Blue Eyes:
Linking Perceptions and Performance
Facilitator Guide

About Us

Indra Lahiri, PhD – the author

Indra Lahiri, Ph.D. is an organizational psychologist, industrial anthropologist and founder of Workforce Development Group. Her clients routinely win national awards for diversity and organizational development efforts. Multi-cultural herself, Dr. Lahiri's personal experience provides her with unique insight into her work. Her teaching experience spans both academic and corporate settings. In addition to **Brown Eyes, Blue Eyes: Linking Perceptions and Performance**, Dr. Lahiri is the author of **Diversity Now: Making Money by Making Sense**, a comprehensive and customizable business case for diversity.

Dr. Lahiri can work with you to customize training programs, lead train-the-facilitator sessions, and work with you on other organizational development projects. Contact her at (215) 453-8577 or write to her at indra@workforcedevelopmentgroup.com.

Workforce Development Group – the producer

Through strategic organizational change strategies, Workforce Development Group has produced measurable results for companies in a variety of industries, as well as government agencies. Their methods have repeatedly:

•Increased productivity
•Decreased turnover
•Improved employee & customer satisfaction
•Increased pool of job applicants

WDG specializes in needs analysis, design and roll-out of inclusive management programs such as mentoring, succession planning, fast-track training, orientation, and employee communications for organizations working toward leveraging diversity to improve bottom line results. Visit our website, www.workforcedevelopmentgroup.com"
www.workforcedevelopmentgroup.com for free tools and resources.

Facilitator Guide

Brown Eyes, Blue Eyes:
Linking Perceptions and Performance
Facilitator Guide

About the Videos

Eye of the Storm

A wake up call for all ages, this best-selling program teaches about prejudice using a dramatic framework. It provides an examination of the realities of discrimination as experienced by actual students in the classroom of third grade teacher, Jane Elliott, whose demonstration shows how quickly children can succumb to discriminatory behavior. The video shows how easily prejudicial attitudes can lead to frustration, broken friendships and vicious behavior. Produced by ABC News. (25 min).

A Class Divided

Filmed 15 years after **Eye of the Storm**, this sequel explores what the children in Jane Elliott's daring classroom experiment learned about discrimination and how it still affects them today. Ms. Elliott meets with some of her former students to analyze the experiment in prejudice and its impact on their lives. In addition, Jane Elliott is seen giving this lesson to employees of the Iowa prison system. Produced by Yale University Films, distributed by PBS Video, a division of the Public Broadcasting Service, (800) 344-3337. (60 minutes).

Angry Eye

Angry Eye is a dynamic and provocative documentary showcasing Jane Elliott's world famous Blue-Eyed/Brown-Eyed exercise in discrimination. The tables are turned on white American college students as they are forced to experience the same kind of racist treatment African Americans and other minorities have been experiencing for years. Produced by Elliott & Elliott Eyes Inc. in association with Pennsylvania Production Associates Inc. Producers: Susan Golenbock and William Talmadge. (Two versions: 35 minutes or 52 minutes).

Essential Blue-Eyed

Many trainers have said the original **Blue Eyed** was the most compelling film on race they had ever seen, but at 86 minutes it was too long. **Essential Blue Eyed** condenses the original film to 50 minutes, and also contains a 36-minute debriefing. Produced by Claus Strigel and Bertram Verhaag.

Facilitator Guide

Brown Eyes, Blue Eyes:
Linking Perceptions and Performance
Facilitator Guide

Table of Contents

Facilitator Guide

Brown Eyes, Blue Eyes:
Linking Perceptions and Performance
Facilitator Guide

Introduction

Facilitating **Brown Eyes, Blue Eyes: Linking Perceptions and Performance** will be both challenging and rewarding. This Facilitator Guide is a tool to walk you through the process, providing you with information, tips, resources and support to help you create a useful learning experience.

Brown Eyes, Blue Eyes: Linking Perceptions and Performance offers a *preliminary introduction* to one important aspect of diversity: the workings of biases, stereotypes and assumptions. The goal of this workshop is to demonstrate how our perceptions about others influence how we treat them, which in turn influences their ability to perform. It enables you to select from several videos that powerfully demonstrate group dynamics. It also illustrates the impact of how we treat each other on productivity and performance. While the videos are informative, they are only the starting point. It is the discussion among participants before and after the video that solidifies learning and transfers new knowledge and insights back to the workplace.

This session will be especially helpful for participants who are:

- Supervisors, team leaders, or managers who have not recently participated in training on diversity

- Not fully living up to the organization's values

- Unclear about the connection between their behavior and the workplace climate

- Newly hired

- Unclear on the organization's definition of, and zero tolerance stance on, discrimination and harassment

- Newly promoted to a supervisory role

Facilitator Guide

Objectives

The objectives of this workshop are to:

- Explore the impact of biases and perceptions on people's feelings, thoughts, and behaviors

- Demonstrate that different treatment leads to differences in performance and productivity

- Encourage participants to think about their roles and responsibilities in relation to the workplace environment

Facilitator Guide

Brown Eyes, Blue Eyes:
Linking Perceptions and Performance
Facilitator Guide

Tools and Materials

You will need the following *materials* to facilitate this session:

☐ **Eye of the Storm, A Class Divided, Angry Eye,** and/or **Essential Blue-Eyed** videotape

☐ Participant Workbooks (1 per participant)

☐ Markers

☐ Masking tape

☐ Name tents (1 per participant)

☐ Sign-in sheet

☐ Extra pens and paper for participants to complete their Action Learning Assignments

☐ **Brown Eyes, Blue Eyes: Linking Perceptions and Performance Facilitator Guide**

Brown Eyes, Blue Eyes:
Linking Perceptions and Performance
Facilitator Guide

You will need the following equipment and room set-up to facilitate this session.

- ☐ TV / VCR

- ☐ Computer, LCD Projector, and Slide Show file OR transparencies with overhead projector

- ☐ Screen

- ☐ Flip chart with easel

- ☐ Clock

- ☐ Tables and chairs arranged in a U-Shape

- ☐ Extra table at side of room for materials

Facilitator Guide

Brown Eyes, Blue Eyes:
Linking Perceptions and Performance
Facilitator Guide

Icons

Simple icons will let you know:

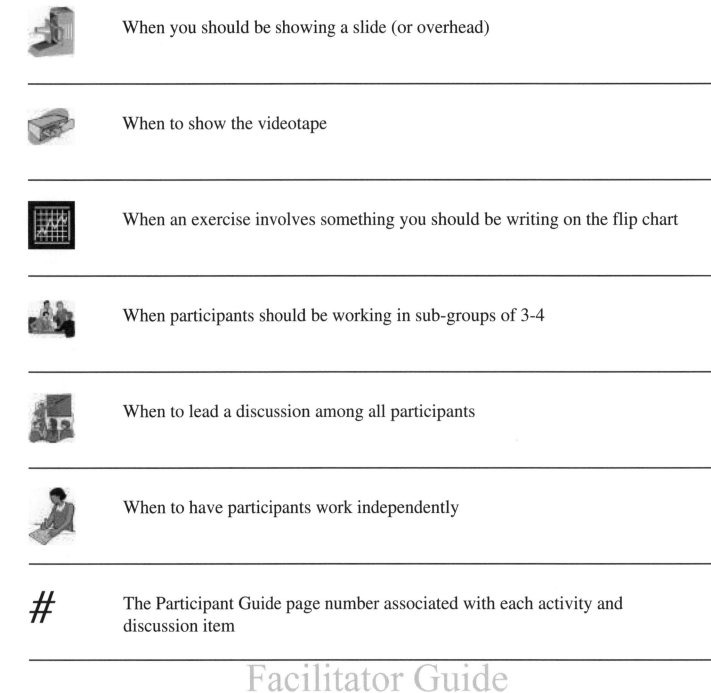

When you should be showing a slide (or overhead)

When to show the videotape

When an exercise involves something you should be writing on the flip chart

When participants should be working in sub-groups of 3-4

When to lead a discussion among all participants

When to have participants work independently

The Participant Guide page number associated with each activity and discussion item

Facilitator Guide

Brown Eyes, Blue Eyes:
Linking Perceptions and Performance
Facilitator Guide

About the Workshop

Brown Eyes, Blue Eyes: Linking Perceptions and Performance offers a *preliminary introduction* to one important aspect of diversity: the workings of biases, stereotypes and assumptions. The goal of this workshop is to demonstrate how our perceptions about others influence how we treat them, which in turn influences their ability to perform. It enables you to select from several videos that powerfully demonstrate group dynamics. You may wish to use **Eye of the Storm, A Class Divided, Angry Eye,** or **Essential Blue-Eyed**. You may choose to use one video for this session and another as a follow-up. Each of these videos illustrates the impact of how we treat each other on productivity and performance. While the videos are informative, they are only the starting point. It is the discussion among participants before and after the video that solidifies learning and transfers new knowledge and insights back to the workplace.

Who should participate?

This workshop is appropriate for businesses, non-profit or government agencies, as well as for use in educational settings. The activities and discussions are designed for adults, yet could easily be modified for teenagers. The key to success in this workshop is to create a safe, comfortable atmosphere in which all participants fully discuss each of the activities, the video, and their thoughts.

How many participants are appropriate?

This workshop is ideally conducted with 10 – 25 participants.

Facilitator Guide

Brown Eyes, Blue Eyes:
Linking Perceptions and Performance
Facilitator Guide

Linkage to Diversity NOW™ Leader Competencies™

Diversity NOW Leader Competencies™ are skills that are required of anyone who wishes to be an effective leader in the 21st century. The full list of competencies, along with a self-assessment and recommended activities to develop each competency, can be found free of charge at www.workforcedevelopmentgroup.com.

Brown Eyes, Blue Eyes: Linking Perceptions and Performance addresses the following Diversity NOW Leader Competencies™:

- **Discernment** – Identifying assumptions based on stereotypes or faulty information that underlie specific actions. Recognizing subtle instances of exclusion.

- **Effective communication** – Listening and hearing with a willingness to be influenced as well as getting your own point across. Communicating effectively with people at all levels in the organization those who report to you, those you report to, peers, customers, and others you work with.

- **Integrity** – Leading by example, role modeling. Advocating appropriately, and in the moment, for those who are excluded.

- **Intellectual energy and curiosity** – Ability and desire to learn from others. Thoughtful contemplation for meaning, co-creation, or breakthrough learning.

- **Mentoring others** – Helping others to succeed through a relationship framed by mutual trust and respect. Sharing your position in relation to others.

Background on Workplace Diversity[1]

What is Diversity?

Diversity is defined as any human difference that distinguishes an individual or group from others. These differences include, for example, age, culture, gender, race, sexual orientation, thinking style, and more.

Any group of people has differences. Diversity is a fact of our lives. Smart organizations know this, and build on those differences to create a climate of inclusion, thereby ultimately enhancing business results.

Diversity in action is how we treat each other. Organizations that are committed to a workplace where everyone is treated respectfully and inclusively are organizations that thrive.

In order to describe diversity initiatives that are grounded in the business, are comprehensive, and inclusive, we will use the term Diversity NOW™. A Diversity NOW Initiative™ is not only about removing barriers. It is about actively making, and living up to, a promise to every unique individual in an organization: "I will not only make it possible for you to succeed, I will go out of my way to make it likely that you do." In exchange (although cynics among us tend to disbelieve it), research shows that most people will work to be the best that they can be, will do the most work, produce the best quality products, offer the best service, and share the most new ideas. This allows companies to make more money.

---

1 Reprinted with permission from 2002. Lahiri, Indra. **Diversity NOW™: Making Money by Making Sense**. Argus, PA: Bullseye Publications.

Facilitator Guide

Brown Eyes, Blue Eyes:
Linking Perceptions and Performance
Facilitator Guide

Abstract principles are important, but concrete results change lives. Therefore, when we refer to a Diversity NOW Initiative™, we are referring to a business strategy designed to:

- Increase market share in growing segments
- Improve team effectiveness
- Attract the most talented and productive people from all backgrounds
- Retain talented and productive employees from all backgrounds
- Provide employees with an environment which allows them to achieve their maximum potential
- Foster mutually beneficial community relationships
- Enhance brand image

The Difference between Diversity and EEO/AAP

Workforce diversity initiatives are separate from legal compliance programs such as Equal Employment Opportunity laws or Affirmative Action plans. These types of programs are important in providing employees with discrimination-free working environments and career opportunities. However, unlike workforce diversity initiatives, compliance programs are not designed to improve corporate bottom line results.

To better understand this distinction, think for a moment about housing.[1] There are laws that prohibit discrimination against those renting or buying housing. Yet, once people move in, there are no laws that say neighbors have to welcome them, invite them to block parties, or even wave to them when passing on the street.

1 This explanation is provided by Sheila Haji, principle of Common Ground Consulting Service (www.commongroundconsulting.com).

Brown Eyes, Blue Eyes:
Linking Perceptions and Performance
Facilitator Guide

EEO laws are like those housing laws. They are important because they ensure that we all have a chance to work without being victimized by discrimination. Diversity and inclusion, though, take an organization further. They are about how individuals are welcomed into the organization, how they are respected and valued. The goal is to create a place where everyone's unique skills are fully used. This way the organization benefits and all employees derive more satisfaction from their work.

With this said, it is important to note that diversity initiatives must create organizational climates that are inclusive and value employees while addressing working conditions as they relate specifically to those traditionally treated as outsiders. It is well documented that women, people of color, people with disabilities, gay, lesbian and bisexual employees, as well as older or very young employees have been treated as outsiders in many organizations. This means that a closer look at each company's workplace environment will reveal both opportunities and challenges regarding utilization of everyone's talents.

In summary, EEO/AAP are federally mandated and legally enforced guidelines barring specific acts of discrimination. Diversity, on the other hand, is a voluntary effort targeted at creating an inclusive and productive work environment.

Inclusion

Effective Diversity NOW Initiatives™ *do not* involve shifting opportunity from one group to another. Rather, they ensure that people of all backgrounds are included, respected, able, and motivated to live up to their full potential.

Diversity NOW Initiatives™ strive to improve team effectiveness and to attract, retain, and develop employees of *all* backgrounds, lifestyles, and cultures. The goal of a Diversity NOW Initiative™ is to be inclusive. In short, this means that organizations must take measures to ensure that all current and potential employees have the same career opportunities and quality work environment, regardless of cultural background, gender, race, or any other differences.

Contrary to common misconceptions, successful workforce diversity initiatives include everyone, and are not designed to limit the opportunities available to any group at the expense of another. In fact, the exclusion of any group can only serve to create missed opportunities and underutilized resources.

Successful Diversity NOW Initiatives™ move beyond simply tolerating one another's differences. They actually capitalize on those differences to enhance productivity, innovation, and customer service. Accordingly, an effective Diversity NOW Strategy™ allows the organization to benefit from every employee's unique talents and perspectives in order to drive profitable growth.

Brown Eyes, Blue Eyes:
Linking Perceptions and Performance
Facilitator Guide

Frequently Asked Questions and Suggested Answers

Following are some common questions regarding diversity and workplace diversity initiatives asked by participants during this workshop. The answers provided are merely suggestions. In all cases, we advocate being honest and genuine. If a suggested answer is not true for your organization, by all means it is best to explain your organization's position.

1.   How are you defining diversity?

Diversity is "human difference that distinguishes an individual or group of people from others. These differences include age, appearance, culture, gender, race, sexual orientation, physical ability, personal and professional style, and other traits." When we talk about diversity, we are talking about all of us.

2.   Why is the organization focusing on diversity now?

The organization will attain our vision and strategic goals only through our people. To support our people in succeeding, we must create a workplace culture that values and supports every employee, business partner, and customer.

In addition, several external driving forces exist, such as:

- Competition for talent and market share

- Changing demographics of the US population

- Continuing need for cost containment through both reducing unnecessary costs (such as unscheduled absenteeism or turnover) and increasing productivity

Facilitator Guide

Brown Eyes, Blue Eyes:
Linking Perceptions and Performance
Facilitator Guide

Facilitator Note: This is an opportunity to share information about the organization's business case for diversity. More information on the business case for diversity, and how to customize it for your organization, is available in **Diversity NOW™: Making Money by Making Sense**, by Indra Lahiri, PhD, 2002.

3.   What are we trying to accomplish?

Through this initiative, we are working toward an organizational climate that not only removes barriers, but actively supports every employee in living up to her or his full potential.

Facilitator Note: This is an opportunity to share the organization's diversity vision and goals.

4.   How is diversity different from EEO/AAP

Workforce diversity initiatives are separate from legal compliance programs such as Equal Employment Opportunity laws or Affirmative Action plans. These types of programs are important in order to provide employees with discrimination-free working environments and career opportunities. However, unlike workforce diversity initiatives, compliance programs are legally mandated, and are not designed to improve bottom line results.

With this said, it is important to note that our diversity initiative must also address working conditions as they relate specifically to those traditionally treated as outsiders. In most American corporations, women, people of color, people with disabilities, gay, lesbian and bisexual employees, as well as older or very young employees have been treated as outsiders. This means that a closer look at our own organizational culture will reveal both opportunities and challenges regarding utilization of the talents of individuals in these and other groups.

Facilitator Guide

5.   How will our diversity initiative affect how we do business?

The diversity initiative does not seek to change the work that we do, but rather to enhance the way that we do it. Through respectful and inclusive interactions supported by system-wide initiatives such as training and mentoring, the way that we do business will be affected. We will all be offered widened opportunities for professional development and career advancement, increased interpersonal effectiveness, and increased employee, manager and customer satisfaction.

6.   What changes can I expect?

That depends on you. What changes will you make in the way that you work with others? Each individual in the organization must make a conscious decision to support her or his colleagues.

Facilitator Note: If your organization has a specific diversity strategy laid out, explain it to participants here.

7.   Will any group be disadvantaged because of our focus on diversity?

No. As the organization continues to move forward with our diversity strategy, we will be careful to monitor the working conditions and opportunities of all employees on the basis of age, physical ability, personal style, organizational level, department, and many other factors in addition to race and gender. The effects of these initiatives, as well as the perspectives of both majority and minority groups, will be considered. In addition, we are committed to ensuring that all tactical steps taken to reach the goal of leveraging diversity will provide opportunities for all employees. We will not employ any method that excludes any group of employees based on their demographic characteristics. Our goal is to create an environment that includes and supports all employees, thus driving profitable growth.

Facilitator Guide

8.   I work in a geographic area that has very little diversity. How does this relate to us?

While many of the areas in which the organization does business are not especially diverse in terms of race, other forms of diversity, such as age, appearance, culture, gender, sexual orientation, personal and professional style, and other traits, exist everywhere we do business. No matter what your geographic area's demographic profile is, the organization is committed to enhancing the workplace environment for all employees.

9.   What benefits will I see from our emphasis on diversity?

In addition to increased opportunities for professional development and career advancement, you will benefit from a work environment that supports and values you as a unique individual.

10.   How will we measure our progress?

We will measure our progress by tracking such things as turnover, numbers and diversity of job applicants and new hires, and data gathered from exit interviews. Additionally, we will be asking for your feedback through an employee satisfaction survey.

Facilitator Note: These are recommendations on how to measure progress. If your organization is doing something different, or not measuring progress at all, be honest with participants.

Facilitator Guide

Difficult Questions with Suggested Answers

Often, facilitators express concern about potentially difficult questions that participants may pose. Following are some questions regarding diversity and workplace diversity initiatives that, during train-the-facilitator sessions, new facilitators voice trepidation about being asked. The answers provided are merely suggestions. In all cases, we advocate being honest and genuine. Again, if a suggested answer is not true for your organization, by all means the best thing to do is explain your organization's position.

1. **What do you, as a man/woman/minority/non-minority/etc., know about diversity?**

Let's remember that our definition of diversity includes everyone, even people like me.

I do not stand here pretending to be anything but what I am, a person who cares about the organization and believes that creating an inclusive, respectful environment will be good for all of us. I do not claim to know all about others' experiences, but that does not mean I don't care or am not willing to learn. I also recognize that others do not know all about my experiences, though I am open to an honest dialogue as a way toward mutual understanding.

Our workforce diversity initiative strives to attract, retain, support, include and develop employees of all backgrounds, lifestyles, and cultures. The goal of a diversity initiative is to be inclusive.

2. **Where do you draw the line when a manager is treating a person of color/a woman/a minority/a gay person more leniently?**

We believe that all employees should be held to the same high standards of performance, and given the same opportunities to improve through honest, direct feedback and support. Withholding feedback or using a double standard is at cross-purposes with the diversity initiative and the organization's policies. It is not good for or fair to the organization or the individual.

Facilitator Guide

3.   What is this program costing us?

Good question, and I do not know exactly what the answer is. Your question, though, does lead to another question, as well. What will it cost us if we do not do this? Diversity initiatives contribute to organizations' profitability through reducing unnecessary costs (like turnover, absenteeism, and legal costs) while increasing morale, improving recruitment efforts, and enhancing customer service. Is this initiative free? No. Would senior management have approved it if it were not a prudently designed initiative that will benefit the business? No. Will it save us money and make us more efficient? It could. That is up to each one of us, and what we do to create an inclusive and respectful workplace.

4.   This sounds like a great idea, but how do I know anything is going to change?

For one thing, the Board of Directors has established a Committee on Diversity that, along with the CEO, asks for, and receives, regular progress reports. They are holding us accountable to make this happen. The CEOs and Senior Leaders each have specific performance expectations related to diversity, and these are tied to their pay. They, in turn, hold the people reporting to them accountable.

I am not saying that this will be easy, and I acknowledge that changing the culture of an organization this large will take time, but our leadership is committed. Now, we need your help.

Facilitator Note: This suggested answer contains our recommendation on tracking the diversity initiative. If your organization is doing something different, or not measuring progress at all, be honest with participants.

---

5.   What do our current statistics show?

They show we are doing well in some areas, and also have a long way to go in others.

6. **Why do I have to be here? Am I in trouble or not considered respectful of diversity?**

All staff, at every level, is going through this training. In addition, CEOs and Senior Leaders are also spending time training on the business case for diversity.

Facilitator Note: This suggested answer contains our recommendation on having employees at every level participate in this workshop. If your organization is doing something different, be honest with participants.

7. **What do we do if a department, area, or individual contradicts the initiative?**

Talk with your manager or human resources representative about your concerns.

8. **How long will it be before we see real change?**

That depends. Culture change, especially in a large, decentralized organization, does not happen overnight. We hope to have some measurable improvements as quickly as a year from now. Other facets of our culture will change over longer periods of time.

9. **I didn't get promoted, and the decision was unfair, let me tell you about it…**
      (or a similar complaint/story)

I can see that this is a serious issue for you. Let's take this conversation off line. After this meeting, I will give you the name of your HR person, who can help you with this situation.

10.   If two people have the exact same competencies, and one is a minority, will the minority get the job?

I can't imagine two people with exactly the same skills, background, and experiences. Managers are being held accountable for providing equal opportunities for all employees and applicants. Our goal here is to widen opportunities, not limit them to one group at the expense of another.

11.   If you are so interested and concerned about diversity, why are you offering "early retirement"?

From time to time, changing business needs cause us to re-evaluate our staffing levels. In the past, we have offered early retirement on a voluntary basis in order to try to meet employees' wishes and meet staffing needs. This is not related to the diversity initiative in any way other than our desire to be fair and inclusive to everyone.

12.   Are you training upper management to be fair to me?

Yes. Not only are all managers, senior leaders, and CEO's attending this training, but also they are being held accountable for supporting diversity, and their pay is tied to their performance in this area. If you have concerns about a specific manager, as always, we encourage you to discuss the issue with your HR person.

Facilitator Note: This suggested answer contains our recommendation for tracking. If your organization is doing something different, be honest with participants.

Facilitator Guide

13. **Most of our senior leadership is white. How can we believe that anything is going to change?**

We recognize that, especially in regard to racial diversity at the top levels, we have a lot of work to do. We are working at recruiting and developing a diverse group of people for top- level positions as they become open. At the same time, we are working at creating a culture that values, respects, includes and supports everyone, so the people we do recruit and promote want to stay with us and are supported in doing their best job.

The Board Committee on Diversity and CEO are overseeing this whole process, and meeting regularly to review our progress as well as support us in continuing to move forward.

Facilitator Note: This suggested answer contains our recommendation on ensuring that real change occurs. If your organization is doing something different, or not measuring progress at all, be honest with participants.

Facilitator Guide

Brown Eyes, Blue Eyes:
Linking Perceptions and Performance
Facilitator Guide

Notes on Group Dynamics

A critical piece of facilitating a successful learning experience is recognizing and managing the group's dynamics. This does not mean that process ought to be elevated over results. Rather, in order to have a good result, a high quality process is necessary.

Your job as a facilitator is to create a safe, inclusive, productive learning environment. If you can do this while focusing on the learning objectives and exploring how participants can apply them at work, you will have a successful session. Here are a few things you can do to create an optimal learning situation:

- Be genuine

- Model inclusive behaviors

- Use group interactions as a learning tool

Following are a few reminders and helpful hints gathered from many talented people who facilitate successful diversity workshops. Feel free to use these, and be sure to share your own tips with others, as well.

Brown Eyes, Blue Eyes:
Linking Perceptions and Performance
Facilitator Guide

Be genuine

Diversity learning is a personal journey. Participants will be more engaged and likely to feel safe if they see you as genuine and true to yourself.

- Share your learning challenges

- Don't be afraid to laugh at yourself

- Take ownership of mistakes

- Demonstrate comfortable and relaxed, yet attentive, body posture, facial expressions, and voice tone

- Use your own words

- Share stories from your work experiences in order to make your points

Model inclusive behavior

Participants learn more from what you do than what you say. For many, inclusive behavior seems like a difficult concept to grasp. By seeing a living example before them, and experiencing how inclusion impacts their performance, you will help them to more clearly grasp the concept.

- Be aware of whom you call on, and whom you do not.

- Check your eye contact. Often, we tend to be more likely to connect with those we expect to connect with.

- Recognize your own privilege as an authority figure, and its impact on the group.

Brown Eyes, Blue Eyes:
Linking Perceptions and Performance
Facilitator Guide

A few words about privilege

Webster's dictionary defines privilege as: 1) A special right, advantage, immunity, permission, right, or benefit granted or enjoyed by an individual or class, or: 2) Such a right or advantage held because of others.

To be able to effectively create a safe and inclusive learning environment, we must be aware of our own privilege. Below are some questions that can help identify examples of privileges that those with the privilege rarely consider. By becoming more aware of our own privileges, we can be better facilitators through understanding the dynamics impacting participants in **Brown Eyes, Blue Eyes: Linking Perceptions and Performance**.

Please note that this list of questions is by no means exhaustive, and is offered simply as examples of the kinds of privileges that are often overlooked unless they are absent.

- Did your parents or caretakers read books to you as a child?

  Having been read to as a child is an advantage not everyone gets to experience. In addition to advancing children educationally, this activity provides children with a sense of caring, which is a powerful feeling.

- Is it safe for you to place a picture of your partner or significant other on your desk at work?

  For many gay and lesbian people, it is politically, if not physically, unsafe for them to display photos similar to the ones that heterosexuals commonly place on their desks.

- In a job interview, do you find the interviewer to be of a different race than you?

  Research shows that those who are more like the interviewer are more at ease, and more likely to be hired. Because the majority of those with hiring power are not people of color, being a non-minority is a privilege in interview situations.

Facilitator Guide

- Have you ever instructed your children or loved ones where to place their hands when their car is stopped by police?

  People of color are more likely than others to be suspected of having weapons when stopped by police. Therefore, some people of color teach their children how to free themselves of this suspicion and thus avoid police thinking they might be armed.

- Have you ever had trouble gaining access to a public place because of a disability?

  For many people with disabilities entering a store, restaurant, or office building can be rife with challenges. These are things that those of us without disabilities often take for granted.

- In order to practice your religious beliefs, do you have to take time off from work?

  Many organizations today still close on Christian holidays, such as Christmas. On other religious holidays, such as Yom Kippur, employees are expected to use vacation time or personal days in order to have time off for worship.

To be effective, facilitators must be aware of their own privileges, and their effects on group dynamics. Consciously creating a safe and inclusive learning environment means not taking the privileges offered to you at another's expense.

For example, a heterosexual facilitator may have no problem referring to her or his spouse causally during the workshop. However, by doing so the facilitator could unconsciously set the stage for a norm of heterosexuality. If a gay or lesbian person feels unsafe already, this can cause him or her to shut down. The same facilitator, by not taking advantage of the privilege, could turn the situation around. For example, he or she could refer to a "partner" instead of a "spouse".

Brown Eyes, Blue Eyes:
Linking Perceptions and Performance
Facilitator Guide

Use group interactions as a learning tool

Often, the very concepts we are discussing play out in the room. For example, participants may denigrate people from another department while discussing what the children in the **Eye of the Storm** video do to make others feel inferior. By pointing these behaviors out, the facilitator can help the group solidify its understanding about the concepts. By facilitating the group in working through their perceptions about employees in the other department, the facilitator can help participants recognize how to apply their learning in their own work.

- Often, in the name of maintaining safety, we fail to hold participants accountable for their learning or their behavior. Yet, some discomfort is an important part of learning.

- Conflict does not necessarily have to be resolved. Common ground can be sought, or the conflict can be a learning opportunity for all.

- Facilitators often mirror the group's feelings. For example, if we feel uncomfortable sharing our own experiences, it is likely that the group does not feel safe either.

- Remember what you are there for. A facilitator cannot solve participants' problems, but we can support them in developing their own problem-solving skills.

Being genuine, modeling inclusive behaviors, and using group interactions as a learning tool are certainly not new concepts to most experienced facilitators. Yet, just as we ask our participants to engage in continuous learning, we can constantly improve on our understanding and mastery of group dynamics.

Facilitator Guide

Before the Session: Laying the Groundwork

Let the department head or manager know that you are planning this session, and what you hope to get out of it. Communicate the importance of each person's full participation in the whole session, from beginning to end. Schedule the workshop for a day that is convenient for all team members. Consider issues such as coverage, flexible time, shifts, etc. Be sure to provide adequate advance notice.

In order to make full use of this time, it is critical to minimize any interruptions. To this end, make it clear to every participant that his or her full attention will be needed for the entire workshop. If participants are not able to commit to this, the session should be postponed until every participant can be fully present.

Choose a location where you will not be disturbed, perhaps in a room that is not located in the same vicinity as participants' workspaces. If possible, arrange for refreshments to be available throughout the session. Keep in mind that participants may have dietary constraints and choose refreshments accordingly. For example, you may have participants that, for religious reasons, are vegetarians or do not eat certain foods. Others may have diabetes or another health condition that requires a specific diet.

Facilitator Guide

Brown Eyes, Blue Eyes:
Linking Perceptions and Performance
Facilitator Guide

Preparing to Facilitate

In preparing to conduct this learning discussion, do the following:

☐ **Read the Facilitator Guide and Participant Guide in their entirety.** Be clear on what you are doing and why, what you want participants doing and when, and how the learning approach works.

☐ **Choose the choose workshop option and the video that you will be using.** This Guide walks you through the process of facilitating:

1. Option I – Full Workshop

2. Option II – Modified Workshop

3. Option III – Abbreviated Workshop

4. Customized Option – Customized Workshop

☐ **Schedule a date, time and location for your learning discussion.** Be sure that you reserve a room large enough for all of your associates, along with a TV / VCR and a screen with an LCD or overhead projector.

☐ **Review past diversity education materials (if any).** Read through your materials from any prior diversity education you or the participants may have attended in the past. Look for opportunities to link learning from this session and prior training.

☐ **Review background information on your organization's diversity initiative.**

Facilitator Guide

Brown Eyes, Blue Eyes:
Linking Perceptions and Performance
Facilitator Guide

☐ **Watch the video(s) you have chosen to use in its entirety.** Each of these videos is a thought-provoking and highly emotional videotape. It will be important that you understand participants' feelings as well as thoughts as they discuss the video. Therefore, it is important for you to be very familiar with the video, and to remember your own emotional reaction as you watched for the first time.

☐ **Study the Facilitator Guide and the accompanying Participant Guide.**

☐ **Make notes for leading the session.**

☐ **Visualize how you will lead the learning discussion.** Think through the flow of events in your mind and note the following points:

    ☐ How you will open the discussion and highlight the importance of diversity.

    ☐ How you will describe the learning approach you plan to take in leading the discussion.

    ☐ The data you will share, to publicly acknowledge and reinforce excellent actions.

    ☐ The points you want to make, and, more importantly, the questions you will ask to stimulate conversation and learning.

    ☐ The examples you will give or solicit to ground the discussion in the real world.

    ☐ The page numbers in the Participant Guide for each participant activity you plan to lead.

Facilitator Guide

Brown Eyes, Blue Eyes:
Linking Perceptions and Performance
Facilitator Guide

☐ **Plan how you will express your expectations for on-the-job application.**

☐ **Plan how you will follow-through and volunteer your support.**

☐ **Gather necessary tools and materials (see "Tools and Materials" list in the Facilitator Guide.)**

Brown Eyes, Blue Eyes:
Linking Perceptions and Performance
Facilitator Guide

The Day of the Workshop

Whenever possible, arrange for a key officer to kick-off the workshop to emphasize the importance of this topic. Suggestions for these opening remarks are included in the section on welcoming participants. Arrive in the training room about an hour before the session is scheduled to begin:

☐ Check that you have all of your materials.

☐ Check that all equipment is in working order, and that you know how to use it.

☐ Place a clock somewhere easy for you to see, so that you can remain on schedule throughout the session.

☐ Depending on the weather, ensure that there is a place for participants' coats, umbrellas, etc.

☐ Ensure that the tables are set up in a U-shape, and that there are enough chairs for the number of participants expected.

☐ Find out where the nearest restrooms are.

☐ Find out how to adjust room temperature and air flow.

☐ Lay out participant workbooks and name tents at each place.

☐ Lay out markers for writing names on the tents (pen is not dark enough to read from across the room.)

Facilitator Guide

Brown Eyes, Blue Eyes:
Linking Perceptions and Performance
Facilitator Guide

☐   Put your own name tent in the front of the room.

☐   Write a large, colorful welcome on the flip chart.

☐   Display the cover slide that shows the workshop title so that participants can verify that they are in the correct place.

Facilitator Guide

Brown Eyes, Blue Eyes:
Linking Perceptions and Performance
Facilitator Guide

Option I: Full Workshop

Learning Objective

- Explore the impact of biases and perceptions on people's feelings, thoughts, and behaviors.

- Demonstrate that different treatment leads to differences in performance and productivity.

- Encourage participants to think about their role and responsibility in relation to the workplace environment.

Facilitator Note: Preview all of the videos and choose the option best for your participants' needs and time constraints. To order video previews, call Trainer's Toolchest 877-288-6657 or you can order previews online www.trainerstoolchest.com.

Agenda (3 - 5.5 hours)

Welcome	15 minutes	page number 43
Why does diversity matter?	30 minutes	page number 50
Video and discussion options (choose one)		
Eye of the Storm	1 hour	page number 56
A Class Divided	2 hours	page number 80
Angry Eye	1.25 hours	page number 89
Essential Blue-Eyed	2.5 hours	page number 99
Break	15 minutes	page number 68
What more can you do?	30 minutes	page number 69
Action learning assignment	20 minutes	page number 74
Wrap up	10 minutes	page number 77

Facilitator Guide

Brown Eyes, Blue Eyes:
Linking Perceptions and Performance
Facilitator Guide

Option II: Modified Workshop

Learning Objectives

- Explore the impact of biases and perceptions on people's feelings, thoughts, and behaviors.

- Demonstrate that different treatment leads to differences in performance and productivity.

- Encourage participants to think about their role and responsibilities in relation to the workplace environment.

Facilitator Note: Preview all of the videos and choose the option best for your participants' needs and time constraints. To order video previews, call Trainer's Toolchest 877-288-6657, or you can order previews online at www.trainerstoolchest.com.

Agenda (1.5 - 3 hours)

Welcome	15 minutes	page number 43
Video and discussion options (choose one)		
Eye of the Storm	1 hour	page number 56
A Class Divided	2 hours	page number 80
Angry Eye	1.25 hours	page number 89
Essential Blue-Eyed	2.5 hours	page number 99
What more can you do?	25 minutes	page number 54
Wrap up	5 minutes	page number 77

Facilitator Guide

Brown Eyes, Blue Eyes:
Linking Perceptions and Performance
Facilitator Guide

Option III: Abbreviated Workshop

Learning Objectives

- Explore the impact of biases and perceptions on people's feelings, thoughts, and behaviors.

- Demonstrate that different treatment leads to differences in performance and productivity.

- Encourage participants to think about their role and responsibility in relation to the workplace environment.

Facilitator Note: Preview all of the videos and choose the option best for your participants' needs and time constraints. To order video previews, call Trainer's Toolchest 877-288-6657, or you can order previews online at www.trainerstoolchest.com.

Agenda (1 - 2.5 hours)

Welcome	10 minutes	page number 43
Video and discussion options (choose one)		
Eye of the Storm	1 hour	page number 56
A Class Divided	2 hours	page number 80
Angry Eye	1.25 hours	page number 89
Essential Blue-Eyed	2.5 hours	page number 99
Wrap up	5 minutes	page number 77

Facilitator Guide

Brown Eyes, Blue Eyes:

Linking Perceptions and Performance
Facilitator Guide

Customized Option: Use this space to create your own workshop

Learning Objectives:

-
-
-
-
-
-
-

Agenda (hours)

minutes	page number
minutes	page number
minutes	page number
minutes	page number
minutes	page number
minutes	page number
minutes	page number

Brown Eyes, Blue Eyes:

Linking Perceptions and Performance
Facilitator Guide

Welcome

Duration	10-15 minutes
Activity Type	Mini-lecture
Segment Flow	
	Facilitator Introduction
	Participant Introductions
	Open the Discussion
	Describe the Learning Approach
	Explain Objectives

Getting Started

The tone you set as participants walk in the door and as you begin the session is critical. Strive for a comfortable, safe learning environment, where mutual respect and lively discussion are the norm. Greet each participant warmly as he or she enters the room. Use appropriate and respectful humor and small talk to help participants feel at ease.

Open up the workshop by introducing yourself and saying a few words about your commitment to helping participants get the most out of this session. Instruct participants to write their names in marker on their name tents, and send the sign-in sheet around the room.

Facilitator Guide

Brown Eyes, Blue Eyes:
Linking Perceptions and Performance
Facilitator Guide

Optional Guest Manager Kick-Off

Whenever possible, arrange for a manager other than the facilitator to kick-off the workshop to emphasize the importance of this topic. Below are suggestions for these opening remarks:

- Thank you for coming. I know how busy you all are, so we do appreciate you taking the time to participate today.

- This workshop concerns a very important topic, the impact of our perceptions about each other on performance.

- This workshop is very interactive, and requires your full participation. Sitting and listening will not allow you to learn what you need to know. I would like you to actively participate by sharing your thoughts, ideas, and questions.

- I went through this workshop myself and gained some important insights from it such as (Share something you learned from the workshop.)

Facilitator Guide

Brown Eyes, Blue Eyes:
Linking Perceptions and Performance
Facilitator Guide

Introductions

Ask participants to introduce themselves by name and by completing the following sentence in three words or less. (Model the introduction by doing so yourself, first.)

"Something you might not guess about me is…"

Pay attention to each introduction. Thank participants, and explain that part of what we will be doing today is learning about not making assumptions. Point out that in the introductions, we learned things about coworkers that we would not necessarily guess by looking at them.

Facilitator Guide

Brown Eyes, Blue Eyes:
Linking Perceptions and Performance
Facilitator Guide

Open the discussion

State your intent for the discussion – what you hope to achieve and how long the discussion will last.

Example of What You Might Say Using **Eye of the Storm**

Today I'd like to talk with you about how we, as human beings, react to differences. We're going to watch a video called **Eye of the Storm**. In 1970, an Iowa teacher named Jane Elliott divided her all-white, all-Christian third graders into blue and brown-eyed groups for a lesson in discrimination none of them would ever forget. This was reality TV long before the concept was coined and marketed. The film reflects clothing, style, and language, even production quality, that may seem outdated by today's standards. However, it is still very relevant to us today, in terms of how our interactions with others can impact productivity and performance. We are scheduled to spend (amount of time) together watching the video and participating in a learning discussion.

Example of What You Might Say Using **A Class Divided**

We're going to watch a video called **A Class Divided.** Filmed 15 years after **Eye of the Storm**, this sequel explores what the children in Jane Elliott's daring classroom experiment learned about discrimination and how it still affects them today. Ms. Elliott meets with some of her former students to analyze the experiment in prejudice and its impact on their lives. In addition, Jane Elliott is seen giving this lesson to employees of the Iowa prison system.

Facilitator Guide

Brown Eyes, Blue Eyes:
Linking Perceptions and Performance
Facilitator Guide

Example of What You Might Say Using **Angry Eye**

We're going to watch a video called **Angry Eye**. In this film white American college students are forced to experience discrimination based on the color of their eyes. As you will see, their experience is very relevant to us today, in terms of how our interactions with others can impact productivity and performance.

Example of What You Might Say Using **Essential Blue-Eyed**

We're going to watch a video called **Essential Blue-Eyed**. In this film adult professionals are forced to experience discrimination based on the color of their eyes. As you will see, their experience is very relevant to us today, in terms of how our interactions with others can impact productivity and performance.

Facilitator Guide

Brown Eyes, Blue Eyes:
Linking Perceptions and Performance
Facilitator Guide

Describe the Learning Approach

Describe your role as facilitator, and their role in teaching each other by sharing their thoughts and learning from each other by listening and asking questions.

Example of What You Might Say

This learning discussion is an opportunity for us to explore our own workplace environment, and how the way we treat each other impacts performance and productivity—either in a constructive way, or in a less positive manner.

This learning discussion is about human nature. No one person is an expert on human nature, of course. So, this is not a session where I can sit here and give you all the answers. Rather, we each have important insights to contribute. The more we all share our thoughts and questions, and the more effectively we listen to each other, the more we will learn. So, I am asking that each of you participate fully in order to make this learning discussion as useful as possible.

Facilitator Guide

Brown Eyes, Blue Eyes:
Linking Perceptions and Performance
Facilitator Guide

Explain Objectives

Objectives: Slide 2

Point out that this session has four parts:

- Discussion on the importance of diversity

- The video

- A learning discussion

- A structured opportunity to implement the skills on the job (the Action Learning Assignment)

# #

Objectives: Participant Guide page 2: Review the learning objectives and the competencies this program supports.

Facilitator Guide

What is Diversity?:
Slide 2

# #

What is Diversity?:
Participant Guide page 3

Why Does Diversity Matter?

Duration	30 minutes
Activity Types	Large group discussion and pairs discussion

Segment Flow

Define Diversity

Why Does Diversity Matter? – Large Group Discussion

How Has Diversity Come Up in Your Work? – Pairs Discussion and Quick Debrief

Define Diversity

Review the definition of diversity by showing slide 3.

Explain how EEO laws differ from diversity. Emphasize that both are important, yet we want to go beyond nondiscrimination and create a climate where everyone is welcome, respected, included, and able to live up to his or her full potential, thus driving the organization's profitable growth.

Brown Eyes, Blue Eyes:
Linking Perceptions and Performance
Facilitator Guide

Why Does Diversity Matter?: Slides 4-6

Why Does Diversity Matter?: Participant Guide pages 4-6

Why Does Diversity Matter? Discussion

One at a time, review the scenario on each slide and solicit 2-3 participant responses as to why diversity matters to the organization.

Acknowledge participants' responses with a nod or a verbal, "Thank you." Repeat participants' responses if necessary to be sure everyone can hear. (Avoid using words like "very good" or "right.")

Scenarios from Slides 4-6 with Possible Responses

Slide # 4 - A customer adheres to an orthodox religious practice of gender segregation in public settings. Why might this matter in terms of how we treat her?

We will need to balance our respect for her practices with our non-discrimination policies. This means we will have to honor her religious practice, yet find ways of ensuring that we do not discriminate on the basis of gender. This scenario would be very different, indeed, if the customer held a prejudice against one gender or another.

Facilitator Guide

Slide # 5 – A new employee is in the minority in terms of his culture, native language, and customs. Why might this matter in terms of how we interact with him?

We need to learn some things about his culture and customs, while teaching him about ours. All of this should be done with great respect. Otherwise, it will be very difficult for him to live up to his full ability, and will in turn impact the whole team's performance. Excellent, two-way communication and an ability to identify cultural clashes, no matter how subtle, as well as the ability to learn about other cultures, will be important for everyone.

Slide # 6 – A community-based organization is committed to continuing education of under-privileged children. Why might this matter to the organization?

As an organization, we must consistently strive to develop our future workforce, enhance our image within the community, and contribute to the community's economic security. For all of these reasons, it makes sense to participate in this endeavor. However, we must be very skilled at working respectfully with all different kinds of people. You see, it is possible for class bias to creep in and undermine this project, unless we make sure that does not happen.

Facilitator Guide

Brown Eyes, Blue Eyes:
Linking Perceptions and Performance
Facilitator Guide

How has diversity come up in your work? Slide 7 and Small Group Discussion

How Has Diversity Come Up in Your Work? – Pairs Discussion and Quick Debrief

Ask participants to pair up with someone sitting nearby and spend 2-3 minutes sharing examples of how diversity has come up in their own work. Be prepared to share a quick example from your own experience to help get things started.

Example of What You Might Say

Let's just spend a moment talking about how diversity shows up for you at work. What I'd like you to do is pair up with someone sitting near you. Talk about an experience you have had with diversity at work. This could be a time you felt different, or worked with someone who is different from you, a coworker, customer, or vendor. What was the difference, and how did it impact the work to be done?

\#

How has diversity come up in your work?: Participant Guide page 7

Facilitator Guide

Brown Eyes, Blue Eyes:

Linking Perceptions and Performance
Facilitator Guide

How Has Diversity Come up in Your Work?: Debrief

Facilitator Note: Be very brief and succinct in this module. The goal is simply to position diversity as a business issue. Do not belabor this point, but move on when it is clear that participants have made the connection.

Ask a few different pairs to summarize their conversation on how diversity has come up for them at work.

Acknowledge participants' responses with a nod or a verbal, "Thank you". Repeat participants' responses if necessary to be sure everyone can hear. (Avoid using words like "very good" or "right".)

Be prepared to share your own thoughts on how diversity shows up at work as well as emphasizing the business benefits of diversity[1] .

---

1 See **Diversity NOW: Making Money by Making Sense** by I. Lahiri (Bullseye Publishing, 2002) for a useful reference on the business benefits of diversity.

Facilitator Guide

Brown Eyes, Blue Eyes:

Linking Perceptions and Performance
Facilitator Guide

# #

**Key Learning Points
About Diversity:
Participant Guide
page 8**

Example of What You Might Say

The organization will attain our vision and strategic goals only through our people. To support our people in succeeding, we must create a workplace culture that values and supports every employee, business partner, and customer.

In addition, several external driving forces exist, such as:

- Competition for talent and market share

- Changing demographics of the US population

- Continuing need for cost containment through both reducing unnecessary costs (such as unscheduled absenteeism or turnover) and increasing productivity

Facilitator Guide

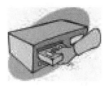

Eye of the Storm

Eye of the Storm Video and Discussion

Duration	60 minutes
Activity Types	Video, small group discussion and large
group debrief	
Segment Flow	
	Introduce and show the video
	Flash reactions
	Small group discussion
	Large group debrief

#

Eye of the Storm Video: Participant Guide page 9

Introduce and show the video

Introduce the video and instruct participants to move to a place where they can watch comfortably. The video itself is about 20 minutes long.

Once the video begins to play, check that the volume level is comfortable for participants in all parts of the room.

Brown Eyes, Blue Eyes:
Linking Perceptions and Performance
Facilitator Guide

Example of What You Might Say

We're going to watch a video called **Eye of the Storm**. In 1970, an Iowa teacher named Jane Elliott divided her all-white, all-Christian third graders into blue and brown-eyed groups for a lesson in discrimination none of them would ever forget. This was reality TV long before the concept of reality TV was coined and marketed. The film reflects clothing, style, and language, and even production quality, that may seem outdated by today's standards. It is, however, very relevant to us today, in terms of how our interactions with others can impact productivity and performance.

Facilitator Note: As the video is playing, some participants may laugh or begin side conversations. Often, these are signs of discomfort. **A small amount of this is normal.**

If, however, you become concerned that participants are not paying attention, or distracting others, simply walk over to the participants who are talking or laughing, and watch the video for a few minutes from that location. Usually, this will cause them to end the distracting behavior.

Facilitator Guide

Brown Eyes, Blue Eyes:
Linking Perceptions and Performance
Facilitator Guide

Flash Reactions to the Video

Flash Reactions to the Video

After the video has ended, tell participants that you recognize that the video is powerful, and that it needs to be discussed. Explain that before discussing it, you would like each person to share a one word thought, feeling, or reaction to the video. (For example, participants might say, "true", "angry", "courage", frightened", etc.)

Facilitator Note: There is no right or wrong response, and no need to discuss reactions further. The point is simply to allow each person to share a reaction.

Facilitator Guide

Brown Eyes, Blue Eyes:
Linking Perceptions and Performance
Facilitator Guide

Eye of the Storm Small Group Discussion: Slide 8

Eye of the Storm Small Group Discussion

Lead the learning discussion by conversing with participants about the video in your natural style. Be sure to encourage different perspectives and to listen to everybody with the intention of learning from them.

- Divide participants into subgroups of 3 or 4 to discuss the questions

- You may wish to assign one question per group if you need to save time

- After about 10 minutes in subgroups, bring the larger group back together and ask them to share highlights of their discussion for each question

- For each question, be sure the learning points provided below are made

- Provide plenty of real-life examples from your experience, and encourage participants to do the same, in order to help participants connect this learning with their job responsibilities

Brown Eyes, Blue Eyes:
Linking Perceptions and Performance
Facilitator Guide

Eye of the Storm discussion questions

Write the Eye of the Storm discussion questions on a flip chart.

Discussion Questions

1. What, specifically, did Jane Elliott do to position the children as inferior or superior?

2. What was the impact on the children's behavior and ability to perform?

3. How, specifically, did the children support or discourage the notion that some are superior and some are inferior?

4. How does this dynamic show up in our workplace?

Brown Eyes, Blue Eyes:
Linking Perceptions and Performance
Facilitator Guide

**Eye of the Storm
Large Group
Debrief**

Eye of the Storm Large Group Debrief

After small groups have had the opportunity to discuss the video, hold a debrief discussion with all participants:

• After about 10 minutes in subgroups, bring the larger group back together

• Ask each subgroup to share highlights of their discussion of the question(s) assigned to them

• After each subgroup shares highlights, ask the rest of the participants if they have questions or would like to add anything

• For each question, be sure that the learning points provided below are made

• Provide plenty of real-life examples from your experience, and encourage participants to do the same, in order to help participants connect this learning with their job responsibilities

Facilitator Guide

Brown Eyes, Blue Eyes:
Linking Perceptions and Performance
Facilitator Guide

Learning Points for Each Discussion Question

1. What, specifically, did Jane Elliott do to position the children as inferior or superior?

Jane Elliott made statements about the groups and backed them up with "facts". For example, she said blue-eyed people are smarter, cleaner, and more civilized than brown-eyed people. She then said that George Washington had blue eyes, and pointed out ways brown-eyed children behaved that were not exemplary. Throughout the day, she reinforced this notion by pointing out examples of when brown-eyed and blue-eyed children lived up to their stereotypes.

Jane Elliott then set up a different set of rules for brown-eyed and blue-eyed children. For example, brown-eyed children were not allowed to: drink from the water fountain without cups, get second helpings at lunch, play on the playground equipment, or play with blue-eyed children. Brown-eyed children were also made to wear collars and sit in the back of the room.

Rules were reversed on the second day, and the blue-eyed children faced the same treatment as brown-eyed children had the day before.

What does this remind you of? The collars may remind people of armbands during the Nazi regime. Many of the rules may remind people of segregation here in the United States.

Jane Elliott's behavior demonstrates how a strong leader can create an inclusive or exclusive environment through creating or enforcing perceptions of ability.

Facilitator Guide

©2002 Indra Lahiri, Ph.D.

2. What was the impact on the children's behavior and ability to perform?

The children were slower at getting through their flash cards on the days they were treated as inferior. The blue-eyed children got through the flash cards in 3 minutes on the day they were treated as superior, and in 4 minutes and 18 seconds when they were treated as inferior. The brown-eyed children got through the flashcards in 5 minutes and 30 seconds on the day they were treated as inferior, and in 2 minutes and 30 seconds on the day they were treated as superior.

Jane Elliott has explained that every child in the class was dyslexic[1]. This further underscores the fact that treatment does affect performance because in that day and age, children with learning disabilities were not even expected to finish school, much less perform as well as these children did when treated as superior.

On the day they were treated as inferior, the children also had distressed looks on their faces, sometimes even looked like they were swearing under their breath, were not paying attention, and generally lacked enthusiasm and energy. One little boy even hit another.

[1] Private telephone conversation between Jane Elliott and the author on July 3, 2002.

Brown Eyes, Blue Eyes:
Linking Perceptions and Performance
Facilitator Guide

If you were observing the classroom on the day the brown-eyed children were treated as inferior, and you did not know about the experiment, what would you think? Would you think the brown-eyed children were smart and well-behaved? What about the blue-eyed children? Would you be right?

Do you think people in your workplace might exhibit poor performance based on the way they are treated, or their perception of the way they are treated? (Offer and solicit examples).

The impact on the children's behavior and ability to perform demonstrates the link between how a person is perceived, the treatment she or he receives as a result of the perception, and the person's performance.

Facilitator Guide

3. How, specifically, did the children support or discourage the notion that some are superior and some are inferior?

In the beginning, a few of the children fought the notion of blue-eyed children being superior. They tried arguing with Jane Elliott, but she always had an answer, and after a few moments even these few stopped arguing.

The children supported the notion not only by following the new rules and not arguing, but also through their own interactions. Do you remember when Jane Elliott couldn't find her yardstick? One of the children had put it on her desk "in case those brown-eyes get out of hand." Another child suggested that Jane Elliott alert the lunchroom help to ensure that the inferior children not be given second helpings at lunchtime.

Do you remember why one little boy hit another ("He called me names and I hit him, hit him in the gut")? Why was the name brown-eyes so upsetting? Because it reminded him of the treatment he received as a result of the label.

Facilitator Guide

Brown Eyes, Blue Eyes:
Linking Perceptions and Performance
Facilitator Guide

Can you think of any examples in our society of words or names that upset people when they are used to describe a group? Do you think this might have to do with the treatment members of that group receive? This can help us to understand why the "politically correct" names for various groups keep changing. The label becomes associated with poor treatment, and starts to feel like an insult. So the name is changed, but the treatment stays the same. Pretty soon the new name is associated with the poor treatment, and it is changed again. We need to change the treatment and then the labels will hurt less.

The children's actions enforcing the perception of one group's superiority over another demonstrate the impact that every individual's behavior has on the workplace environment, and ultimately on performance.

Facilitator Guide

What can you, personally, do to address these dynamics?

Key Learning Points About My Responsibility with Regard to Diversity: Participant Guide page 11

# #

Key Learning Points from Video:Participant Guide page 12

4. How does this dynamic show up in our workplace?

Are there certain departments that seem to be treated as superior or inferior? (Be prepared to provide some examples.)

Who succeeds in this organization? Is there a specific profile, perhaps to do with schools people went to, personality style, or a certain look that is associated with success? Who might not succeed? Why?

Be prepared to push for specific, concrete actions to address these dynamics. Write participants' and your own ideas down on a flip chart.

Example of What You Might Say

Here is the most important question: What can you, personally, do to address these dynamics in the workplace?

Facilitator Guide

Break (15 minutes)

Be sure to point out where the restrooms are, and be specific about what time the workshop will reconvene. Often, mentioning that you want to be sure to end the session on time provides participants with incentive to return on time.

Brown Eyes, Blue Eyes:
Linking Perceptions and Performance
Facilitator Guide

# #

What More Can You Do?: Participant Guide pages 13-28

What More Can You Do?

Duration	30 minutes
Activity Type	Large group discussion
Segment Flow	

For each scenario:
    Introduce scenario on slide
    Solicit participant suggestions
    Elaborate briefly on suggestions from
    the follow-up slide

This activity consists of presenting eight different situations related to diversity in the workplace that participants are likely to face through the course of their work. Each of these situations has an accompanying slide with suggested actions participants can take to respond inclusively.

Facilitator Guide

Brown Eyes, Blue Eyes:
Linking Perceptions and Performance
Facilitator Guide

What More Can You Do?: Large Group Discussion: Slides 9-24

For each slide with a scenario:

- Review scenario, and make small comments as appropriate to keep the workshop flowing naturally. (For example, "This is a really common one.")

- Solicit 2-3 participants' responses to the question.

- Repeat participants' responses if necessary to be sure everyone can hear.

- Acknowledge responses with a nod or a verbal, "Thank you."

For each slide with recommended responses to the scenario:

- Acknowledge suggestions made by participants that are on the slide.

- Review additional suggestions on the slide.

- Add your own thoughts on additional things participants could do in this situation as appropriate.

Facilitator Guide

Brown Eyes, Blue Eyes:
Linking Perceptions and Performance
Facilitator Guide

Facilitator Note: The goal of this activity is not simply to tell participants how to respond, but to get them thinking about the situations and encourage them to recognize the many ways they each contribute to their own workplace environment.

Keep this discussion succinct and involve participants through questions and answers as much as possible. At the same time, avoid being too brief as this would allow participants to finish the activity without thinking through the scenarios.

Avoid getting into a conversation with one group or participant to the exclusion of others.

Feel free to provoke the group into thinking through creative and realistic approaches to the scenarios to keep the dialogue productive and engaging. As soon as the necessary points have been made, move on.

Brown Eyes, Blue Eyes:
Linking Perceptions and Performance
Facilitator Guide

What More Can You Do? Scenarios

These are the scenarios that appear on the slides for this segment:

- Sharice, a new employee, eats lunch alone everyday. What can you do?

- Ms. D'Onofrio, a customer, seems confused but does not ask any questions. What can you do?

- On the telephone, you are having trouble understanding a customer who speaks English with an accent. What can you do?

- Two co-workers are making stereotypical comments about an employee from another ethnic background. What can you do?

- You work in a geographic area that has very little diversity. What can you do?

- You hear that the diversity council is partnering with community groups to sponsor various events. What can you do?

- You are the manager of a team of 6 people. Several of the team members have been grumbling that the most senior person on the team is being given special treatment. The team members complain that the senior person is often allowed to leave work early or come in late. What can you do?

Facilitator Guide

Brown Eyes, Blue Eyes:
Linking Perceptions and Performance
Facilitator Guide

- You have just hired a person of a different racial background than any other members of your team. You want to set this person up for success equal to the other team members. You recognize that there will be challenges, many of them subtle, to overcome. What can you do?

Action Learning Assignment: Slides 25-28

Action Learning Assignment: Participant Guide pages 29-30

Action Learning Assignment

Duration   20 minutes
Activity Type   Individual Activity
Segment Flow

Introduce assignment
Provide examples of types of activities
Participants complete assignment
Solicit one example from each participant

Tell participants that the workshop is nearing its end. Ask them to take a few moments to focus on what they have learned and how they will use the knowledge by completing the Action Learning Assignment.

Describe the Action Learning Assignment and the behaviors you expect participants to demonstrate on the job.

Brown Eyes, Blue Eyes:
Linking Perceptions and Performance
Facilitator Guide

Example of What You Might Say

So here is what I'd like each one of you to do between now and (date). Consider the list we just came up with, things we can do to address the dynamics we saw in the film. Come up with target actions that you can focus on immediately to make a difference. These would be actions that:

- Seek out and use ideas, opinions, and insights from diverse and various sources

- Maximize effectiveness by using individuals' particular talents and abilities on tasks or assignments

- Recruit and/or develop individuals from various backgrounds and cultures

- Confront racist, sexist, or inappropriate behavior from others

- Challenge exclusionary practices

- Create an environment where differences and similarities are shared and celebrated

- Encourage others to seek out knowledge about differences

- Strive for understanding of differences

- Learn to view differences and similarities as strengths to be leveraged

Facilitator Guide

Brown Eyes, Blue Eyes:
Linking Perceptions and Performance
Facilitator Guide

- Examine your own behavior towards those who are different from you or toward alternative ideas

As a result of this reflection, you should be able to:

- Clearly state some deliberate actions you are taking to leverage diversity with co-workers

- Find ways to use the unique strengths and talents of your team in ways you previously have not tried

- Gather feedback from others concerning your ability to interact with a variety of colleagues

Facilitator Guide

Wrap Up

Duration   10 minutes
Activity Types   Mini-lecture and Participant Evaluations

Segment Flow

Clarify expectations
Offer ongoing help and support
Thank participants
Participants complete evaluations and ac
knowledgments

Clarify expectations

Clarify your expectations. State follow-through actions for
additional learning and accountability.

Example of What You Might Say

As you take action, note what happens. We'll report our learning when we get together on (date). At that time, we'll discuss
what went well, and what we would do differently.

Facilitator Guide

Brown Eyes, Blue Eyes:

Linking Perceptions and Performance
Facilitator Guide

Offer ongoing support and help

After the learning discussion, be sure to follow up with each participant to ensure that they are completing their Action Learning Assignment. Bring the whole group together a month or two later to discuss their Action Learning Assignment and share their learning.

Assure participants that you will continue to support them in applying their learning in the months to come.

Encourage all participants to continue their learning on this topic. Identify any internal learning resources your company provides. Point out that many opportunities for ongoing education through free articles, assessments, learning tools, and links to useful web sites, as well as recommendations on videos and books that are available through www.workforcedevelopmentgroup.com.

Example of What You Might Say

If any of you would like more clarity on the things we discussed today or the diversity initiative, please let me know. If there are other questions you have, or ways I can assist you going forward, don't hesitate to ask.

We will be meeting again as a group on (date) to discuss how our Action Learning Assignments went, and to share what we have learned. This is a good opportunity to coach and support each other. In the meantime, I will be checking in with each of you individually to see how things are going and give you any help that you need.

Facilitator Guide

Brown Eyes, Blue Eyes:
Linking Perceptions and Performance
Facilitator Guide

Participant Evaluations and Acknowledgments pages 31-32

Evaluations and Close

Thank participants for their involvement, and share something positive you observed about this group. Emphasize how and where any questions that arise in the future can be addressed.

Instruct participants to complete their Participant Evaluations and Acknowledgments which are on pages 31-32. Designate a place in the room for participants to place completed evaluations, and let them know they can leave after turning in the evaluation. Ask participants to tear out their Evaluations and Acknowledgments from their Participant Guide, so they may turn them into you and keep their Participant Guide.

Collect and forward evaluations and acknowledgments as appropriate for your organization. Use feedback from participants to adjust your approach the next time you facilitate a learning discussion.

Facilitator Guide

A Class Divided Video and Discussion

Facilitator Note: You may wish to use **Eye of the Storm** as in the initial workshop, then bring participants back together at a later date to watch and discuss **A Class Divided.**

A Class Divided is longer than **Eye of the Storm**, focuses more sharply on race and racism, and is therefore sometimes perceived as more intense. For these reasons, participants are more likely to react to this film with highly charged emotions, including grief or anger. The facilitator's responsibility is to take care of participants, including fully debriefing them and balancing emotions with specific and applicable learning points. If you are not a professional at facilitating volatile topics, or if you are not ready to live up to this responsibility, do not attempt to facilitate this session. Instead, find a qualified professional and use this as an opportunity to further develop your facilitation skills by learning from her or him.

Duration	2 hours
Activity Types	Video, small group discussion and large group debrief
Segment Flow	
	Introduce and show the video
	Flash reactions
	Small group discussion
	Large group debrief

Brown Eyes, Blue Eyes:
Linking Perceptions and Performance
Facilitator Guide

A Class Divided

Introduce and show the video

Introduce the video and instruct participants to move to a place where they can watch comfortably. The video itself is about 60 minutes long.

Once the video begins to play, check that the volume level is comfortable for participants in all parts of the room.

Example of What You Might Say

We're going to watch a video called **A Class Divided.** Filmed 15 years after **Eye of the Storm**, this sequel explores what the children in Jane Elliott's daring classroom experiment learned about discrimination and how it still affects them today. Ms. Elliott meets with some of her former students to analyze the experiment in prejudice and its impact on their lives. In addition, Jane Elliott is seen giving this lesson to employees of the Iowa prison system.

Facilitator Guide

Brown Eyes, Blue Eyes:

Linking Perceptions and Performance
Facilitator Guide

Facilitator Note: As the video is playing, some participants may cry, laugh, or begin side conversations. Often, these are signs of discomfort. **A small amount of this is normal.**

If, however, you become concerned that participants are in need of help, not paying attention, or distracting others, simply walk over to the participants who are crying, talking or laughing, and watch the video for a few minutes from that location. Usually, this will cause them to end the distracting behavior. A hand on the back of the chair, or a whispered "Are you okay?", is appropriate if a participant is crying.

Use your judgment in helping participants through more extreme emotional reactions.

Facilitator Guide

Brown Eyes, Blue Eyes:
Linking Perceptions and Performance
Facilitator Guide

Flash Reactions to the Video

Flash Reactions to the Video

After the video has ended, tell participants that you recognize that the video is powerful, and that it needs to be discussed. Explain that before discussing it, you would like each person to share a one word thought, feeling, or reaction to the video. (For example, participants might say, "true", "angry", "courage", frightened", etc.)

Facilitator Note: There is no right or wrong response, and no need to discuss reactions further. The point is simply to allow each person to share a reaction.

Facilitator Guide

Brown Eyes, Blue Eyes:
Linking Perceptions and Performance
Facilitator Guide

A Class Divided Small Group Discussion

A Class Divided Small Group Discussion

Lead the learning discussion by conversing with participants about the video in your natural style. Be sure to encourage different perspectives and to listen to everybody with the intention of learning from them.

- Print the discussion questions below on a flip chart

- Divide participants into subgroups of 3 or 4 to discuss the questions

- You may wish to assign one or two questions per group if you need to save time

- After about 10 minutes in subgroups, bring the larger group back together and ask them to share highlights of their discussion for each question

- For questions 1-5, be prepared to offer examples from the video to make the point that how we perceive others impacts how we treat them, and how we treat others impacts how they perform

- Questions 6-10 ask participants to share personal reactions and experiences. For these questions, remember that there are no right or wrong answers, and focus on learning from each person

- Provide plenty of real-life examples from your experience, and encourage participants to do the same, in order to help participants connect this learning with their job responsibilities

Facilitator Guide

Brown Eyes, Blue Eyes:
Linking Perceptions and Performance
Facilitator Guide

Discussion Questions

Discussion Questions

Discussion Questions

1. Jane Elliott indicates in this video that, after her brown eyes/blue eyes exercise with the children as third-graders, the children's grades improved. Why do you think that is?

2. What does this tell us about opportunities we may have in the workplace?

3. How, specifically, can leaders in your organization improve employee's performance? How can individual performers improve each other's performance?

4. Why didn't the blue-eyes in the correctional facility just go into the classroom when one man suggested it? Why didn't they object to the treatment they received?

5. What, specifically, did Jane Elliott do to set the dynamic of exclusion?

6. Did the discussion between the classmates and Jane Elliott hold any surprises for you?

7. How did it feel to watch this? Why?

8. Have you ever seen a leader do something similar? What happened?

Facilitator Guide

9. How has seeing the reunion impacted your perspective on Jane Elliott's initial brown eyes/blue eyes exercise with her 3rd grade class?

10. Have you ever seen people "living down to their expectation" in the workplace? How can this be changed?

Brown Eyes, Blue Eyes:
Linking Perceptions and Performance
Facilitator Guide

A Class Divided Large Group Debrief

A Class Divided Large Group Debrief

After small groups have had the opportunity to discuss the video, hold a debrief discussion with all participants:

- After about 10 minutes in subgroups, bring the larger group back together

- Ask each subgroup to share highlights of their discussion of the question(s) assigned to them

- After each subgroup shares highlights, ask the rest of the participants if they have questions or would like to add anything

- For questions 1-5, be prepared to offer examples from the video to make the point that how we perceive others impacts how we treat them, and how we treat others impacts how they perform

- Questions 6-10 ask participants to share personal reactions and experiences. For these questions, remember that there are no right or wrong answers and focus on learning from each person

- Provide plenty of real-life examples from your experience, and encourage participants to do the same, in order to help participants connect this learning with their job responsibilities

Facilitator Guide

Brown Eyes, Blue Eyes:
Linking Perceptions and Performance
Facilitator Guide

Learning Points

During the discussion, be sure that the following learning points are addressed:

- People's perceptions of others are influenced by a leader's behavior

- We all send messages about whether we think a person is inferior or superior not just through what we say and do not say, but also through voice tone, body language, eye contact or lack thereof, how we arrange and decorate the room, and in many other very subtle ways

- People who are treated as inferior have trouble with even the simplest tasks (as in repeating a few rules for good listeners in the video). This is true for children and adults alike

- The way we treat others is therefore directly linked to their performance

- We are all responsible for our own performance, yet those who are treated as inferior have unnecessary barriers that are always difficult, and sometimes impossible, to overcome

Facilitator Guide

Brown Eyes, Blue Eyes:
Linking Perceptions and Performance
Facilitator Guide

Angry Eye Video and Discussion

Facilitator Note: **Angry Eye** is more current than **Eye of the Storm** or **A Class Divided.** It also focuses more sharply on race and racism, and is therefore more intense. For these reasons, participants are more likely to react to this film with highly charged emotions, including grief or anger. The facilitator's responsibility is to take care of the participants, including fully debriefing them and balancing their emotions with specific and applicable learning points. If you are not a professional at facilitating volatile topics, or if you are not ready to live up to this responsibility, do not attempt to facilitate this session. Instead, find a qualified professional and use this as an opportunity to further develop your facilitation skills by learning from her or him.

Duration	90 minutes
Activity Types	Video, small group discussion and large group debrief
Segment Flow	
	Introduce and show the video
	3 Words
	Small group discussion
	Large group debrief

Facilitator Guide

Brown Eyes, Blue Eyes:

Linking Perceptions and Performance
Facilitator Guide

Angry Eye

Introduce and show the video

Introduce the video and instruct participants to move to a place where they can watch comfortably. The video itself is about 35 minutes.

Facilitator Note: There are two versions of Angry Eye available; one is 35 minutes, and the other is 52 minutes. The time frames shown here reflect the 35 minute version. If you choose to use the 52-minute version, remember to add 17 minutes to the time for the video and discussion.

Once the video begins to play, check that the volume level is comfortable for participants in all parts of the room.

Example of What You Might Say

We're going to watch a video called **Angry Eye**. In this film white American college students are forced to experience discrimination based on the color of their eyes. As you will see, their experience is very relevant to us today, in terms of how our interactions with others can impact productivity and performance.

Facilitator Guide

Brown Eyes, Blue Eyes:
Linking Perceptions and Performance
Facilitator Guide

Facilitator Note: As the video is playing, some participants may cry, laugh, or begin side conversations. Often, these are signs of discomfort. **A small amount of this is normal.**

If, however, you become concerned that participants are in need of help, not paying attention, or distracting others, simply walk over to the participants who are crying, talking or laughing, and watch the video for a few minutes from that location. Usually, this will cause them to end the distracting behavior. A hand on the back of the chair, or a whispered "Are you okay?", is appropriate if a participant is crying.

Use your judgment in helping participants through more extreme emotional reactions.

Facilitator Guide

Brown Eyes, Blue Eyes:
Linking Perceptions and Performance
Facilitator Guide

3 Words

3 Words

After the video has ended, tell the participants you recognize that the video is powerful and that it needs to be discussed. Explain that before discussing it, you would like each person to write down:

- 3 words to describe blue-eyed people in the video

- 3 words to describe brown-eyed people in the video

- 3 words to describe how they felt watching the video

Hang two flipcharts on the wall. Ask participants to walk up to the first flipchart and write 1-3 words to describe blue-eyed people, then ask them to write words to describe brown-eyed people on another flipchart. As you are waiting for everyone to finish this, ask participants to share the words they chose to describe how they felt watching the video.

Ask participants to read the lists and choose which group of people they would rather have working for them.

Brown Eyes, Blue Eyes:

Linking Perceptions and Performance
Facilitator Guide

Facilitator Note: There is no right or wrong response to how people felt while watching the film, and no need to discuss reactions further. The point is simply to allow each person to share a reaction.

The point of listing descriptions of brown-eyed and blue-eyed people is to demonstrate how treatment affected their demeanor and behavior.

Facilitator Guide

Brown Eyes, Blue Eyes:
Linking Perceptions and Performance
Facilitator Guide

Angry Eye Small Group Discussion

Angry Eye Small Group Discussion

Lead the learning discussion by conversing with participants about the video in your natural style. Be sure to encourage different perspectives and to listen to everybody with the intention of learning from them.

- Print the discussion questions below on a flip chart

- Divide participants into subgroups of 3 or 4 to discuss the questions

- You may wish to assign one or two questions per group if you need to save time

- After about 10 minutes in subgroups, bring the larger group back together and ask them to share highlights of their discussion for each question

- Be prepared to offer examples from the video to make the point that how we perceive others impacts how we treat them, and how we treat others impacts how they perform

- Some of the questions ask participants to share personal reactions and experiences. For these questions, remember that there are no right or wrong answers, and focus on learning from each person

- Provide plenty of real-life examples from your experience, and encourage participants to do the same, in order to help participants connect this learning with their job responsibilities

Facilitator Guide

Brown Eyes, Blue Eyes:
Linking Perceptions and Performance
Facilitator Guide

Discussion Questions

Discussion Questions

1. Do you think it is possible to be "color-blind"? Why or why not?

2. Why do some people in the video seem angry at being told, "I don't see you as Black?" Why might a person say they do not see someone as the race they are?

3. How did Jane Elliott's treatment impact participants' performance?

4. How did the arrangement of chairs and the posters around the room contribute to setting blue-eyed people up as inferior?

5. How did others' laughter contribute?

6. Why do you think two of the women cried when they tried to defend themselves?

7. What do you think of Jane Elliott's assertion that the woman who left the room asserted a right that others don't have? Can you think of other examples of some people asserting rights that others do not have?

8. Where else have you seen the dynamics from this film played out?

Facilitator Guide

9. What do you think of Carrie's feeling that she can understand what Black people go through? Is this possible? Why or why not?

10. Jane Elliott, in speaking of one participant, said that he came away with an understanding of how power works. After watching this film, how do you think power works?

Brown Eyes, Blue Eyes:
Linking Perceptions and Performance
Facilitator Guide

Angry Eye Large Group Debrief

Angry Eye Large Group Debrief

After small groups have had the opportunity to discuss the video, hold a debrief discussion with all participants:

- After about 10 minutes in subgroups, bring the larger group back together

- Ask each subgroup to share highlights of their discussion of the question(s) assigned to them

- After each subgroup shares highlights, ask the rest of the participants if they have questions or would like to add anything

- Be prepared to offer examples from the video to make the point that how we perceive others impacts how we treat them, and how we treat others impacts how they perform

- Some of the questions ask participants to share personal reactions and experiences. For these questions, remember that there are no right or wrong answers, and focus on learning from each person

- Provide plenty of real-life examples from your experience, and encourage participants to do the same, in order to help participants connect this learning with their job responsibilities

Facilitator Guide

Brown Eyes, Blue Eyes:
Linking Perceptions and Performance
Facilitator Guide

Learning Points

During the discussion, be sure the following learning points are made:

- Prejudice is often the *result* of discrimination. For example, when the blue-eyed people in the video were treated as inferior, they began to have difficulty performing even simple tasks requested by Jane Elliott. Others then see this behavior and conclude that a group of people is inferior, and become prejudiced

- Oppression, such as we saw in the film, often leads to "learned helplessness". The blue-eyed people saw that any attempts to refute their inferiority were met with even harsher treatment, and quickly stopped trying to help themselves or each other

- If Jane Elliott was able to cause these people to live down to her expectations through her treatment of them, it is also possible to treat others in a supportive and encouraging way, causing them to live up to our expectations

Facilitator Guide

Brown Eyes, Blue Eyes:

Linking Perceptions and Performance
Facilitator Guide

Essential Blue-Eyed Video and Discussion

Facilitator Notes: Essential Blue-Eyed is more current than **Eye of the Storm** or **A Class Divided**. It is also longer, focuses more sharply on race and racism, and is therefore more intense. For these reasons, participants are more likely to react to this film with highly charged emotions, including grief or anger. The facilitator's responsibility is to take care of participants, including fully debriefing the experience and balancing emotions with specific and applicable learning points. If you are not a professional at facilitating volatile topics, or if you are not ready to live up to this responsibility, do not attempt to facilitate this session. Instead, find a qualified professional and use this as an opportunity to further develop your facilitation skills by learning from her or him.

Duration	3 hours
Activity Types	Video, small group discussion and large group debrief
Segment Flow	
	Introduce and show the video
	3 Words
	Small group discussion
	Large group debrief
	Video and Discussion

Facilitator Guide

Brown Eyes, Blue Eyes:

Linking Perceptions and Performance
Facilitator Guide

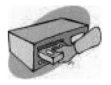

Essential Blue-Eyed

Introduce and show the video

Introduce the video and instruct participants to move to a place where they can watch comfortably. The video itself is about 90 minutes long.

Once the video begins to play, check that the volume level is comfortable for participants in all parts of the room.

Example of What You Might Say

We're going to watch a video called **Essential Blue-Eyed**. In this film adult professionals are forced to experience discrimination based on the color of their eyes. As you will see, their experience is very relevant to us today, in terms of how our interactions with others can impact productivity and performance.

Facilitator Guide

Brown Eyes, Blue Eyes:
Linking Perceptions and Performance
Facilitator Guide

Facilitator Note: As the video is playing, some participants may cry, laugh, or begin side conversations. Often, these are signs of discomfort. **A small amount of this is normal.**

If, however, you become concerned that participants are in need of help, not paying attention, or distracting others, simply walk over to the participants who are crying, talking or laughing, and watch the video for a few minutes from that location. Usually, this will cause them to end the distracting behavior. A hand on the back of the chair, or a whispered "Are you okay?", is appropriate if a participant is crying.

Use your judgment in helping participants through more extreme emotional reactions.

Facilitator Guide

Brown Eyes, Blue Eyes:
Linking Perceptions and Performance
Facilitator Guide

3 Words

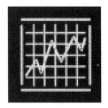

3 Words

After the video has ended, tell participants that you recognize that the video is powerful, and that it needs to be discussed. Explain that before discussing it, you would like each person to write down:

- 3 words to describe blue-eyed people in the video

- 3 words to describe brown-eyed people in the video

- 3 words to describe how they felt watching the video

Hang two flipcharts on the wall. Ask participants to walk up to the first flipchart and write 1-3 words to describe blue-eyed people, then ask them to write words to describe brown-eyed people on another flipchart. As you are waiting for everyone to finish this, ask participants to share the words they chose to describe how they felt watching the video.

Ask participants to read the lists and choose which group of people they would rather have working for them.

Facilitator Guide

Brown Eyes, Blue Eyes:
Linking Perceptions and Performance
Facilitator Guide

Facilitator Note: There is no right or wrong response to how people felt while watching the film, and no need to discuss reactions further. The point is simply to allow each person to share a reaction.

The point of listing descriptions of brown-eyed and blue-eyed people is to demonstrate how treatment affected their demeanor and behavior.

Facilitator Guide

Brown Eyes, Blue Eyes:
Linking Perceptions and Performance
Facilitator Guide

**Essential Blue-Eyed
Small Group Discussion**

Essential Blue-Eyed Small Group Discussion

Lead the learning discussion by conversing with participants about the video in your natural style. Be sure to encourage different perspectives and to listen to everybody with the intention of learning from them.

- Print the discussion questions below on a flip chart

- Divide participants into subgroups of 3 or 4 to discuss the questions

- You may wish to assign one or two questions per group if you need to save time

- After about 10 minutes in subgroups, bring the larger group back together and ask them to share highlights of their discussion for each question

- Be prepared to offer examples from the video to make the point that how we perceive others impacts how we treat them, and how we treat others impacts how they perform

- Some of the questions ask participants to share personal reactions and experiences. For these questions, remember that there are no right or wrong answers, and focus on learning from each person

- Provide plenty of real-life examples from your experience, and encourage participants to do the same, in order to help participants connect this learning with their job responsibilities

Facilitator Guide

Brown Eyes, Blue Eyes:
Linking Perceptions and Performance
Facilitator Guide

Discussion Questions

Discussion Questions

1. How does Jane Elliott use body language and voice tone to convey whether others are inferior or superior?

2. Why did the blue-eyed people not revolt even before entering the room?

3. Do you agree with Jane Elliott that people of color are treated the way that she treats blue-eyed people? Why or why not?

4. Do you agree with Jane Elliott that you need to "act white to get ahead?" Why or why not?

5. How did blue-eyed people respond to the treatment they received (voice, body language, facial expressions, behavior)? If you saw someone acting that way at work, what would you think of him or her?

6. Do you agree that society makes some groups "live down to their expectations?" Why or why not?

7. Do you believe we can encourage people to live up to high expectations? How?

8. What purpose did the posters and collars serve?

Facilitator Guide

9. What did the photos from the children in **Essential Blue-Eyed** tell you? Did you see this in the adults from this film? Does this translate into performance? How?

10. Jane Elliott states that "to sit back and do nothing is to aid the oppressor." If so, what can you do?

Brown Eyes, Blue Eyes:
Linking Perceptions and Performance
Facilitator Guide

**Essential Blue-Eyed
Large Group Debrief**

Essential Blue-Eyed Large Group Debrief

After small groups have had the opportunity to discuss the video, hold a debrief discussion with all participants:

- After about 10 minutes in subgroups, bring the larger group back together

- Ask each subgroup to share highlights of their discussion of the question(s) assigned to them

- After each subgroup shares highlights, ask the rest of the participants if they have questions or would like to add anything

- Be prepared to offer examples from the video to make the point that how we perceive others impacts how we treat them, and how we treat others impacts how they perform

- Some of the questions ask participants to share personal reactions and experiences. For these questions, remember that there are no right or wrong answers, and focus on learning from each person

- Provide plenty of real-life examples from your experience, and encourage participants to do the same, in order to help participants connect this learning with their job responsibilities

Facilitator Guide

Brown Eyes, Blue Eyes:
Linking Perceptions and Performance
Facilitator Guide

Learning Points

Be sure that the following learning points are made during the discussion:

- Every human being has the capacity to discriminate or be discriminated against

- Discrimination occurs when a person is treated as inferior due to group membership or a specific characteristic over which the person has no control

- When we perceive others as inferior, it shows through our facial expressions, body language, voice tone, and other subtle behaviors. This has a profound impact on those receiving the treatment

- Prejudice is often the *result* of discrimination. For example, when the blue-eyed people in the video were treated as inferior, they began to have difficulty performing even simple tasks requested by Jane Elliott. Others then see this behavior and conclude that a group of people is inferior, and become prejudiced

- Oppression, such as we saw in the film, often leads to "learned helplessness". The blue-eyed people saw that any attempts to refute their inferiority were met with even harsher treatment, and quickly stopped trying to help themselves or each other

Facilitator Guide

Brown Eyes, Blue Eyes:

Linking Perceptions and Performance
Facilitator Guide

- If Jane Elliott was able to cause these people to live down to her expectations through her treatment of them, it is also possible to treat others in a supportive and encouraging way, causing them to live up to our expectations

- Each individual can and should make a difference in eliminating "isms"

Speaker Notes and Slide Examples

On the following pages are printed examples of each slide with the accompanying speaker notes that we suggest you use while showing the slides. We have provided additional space for your own speaker notes on each slide page.

Brown Eyes, Blue Eyes:
Linking Perceptions and Performance
Facilitator Guide

Slide 1

Brown Eyes, Blues Eyes:
Linking Perceptions
and Performance

©2002 Workforce Development Group

Speaker Notes

"Welcome! Thank you for being here with us to talk about perceptions and productivity. Before we begin, I'd like to turn the floor over to _____ (CEO/SeniorLeader/Diversity Council member), who wants to talk to you about this workshop."

Guest speaker:

- States personal and organizational commitment to this effort

- Underscores the need for each participant's involvement in the initiative to make it a success

- Encourages participants to engage in dialogue and ask questions

Brown Eyes, Blue Eyes:
Linking Perceptions and Performance
Facilitator Guide

Slide 2

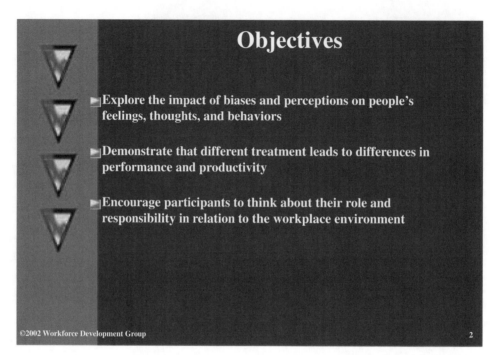

Objectives

▶ Explore the impact of biases and perceptions on people's feelings, thoughts, and behaviors

▶ Demonstrate that different treatment leads to differences in performance and productivity

▶ Encourage participants to think about their role and responsibility in relation to the workplace environment

©2002 Workforce Development Group   2

Speaker Notes

Read objectives out loud, using your own words if this is more comfortable.

Facilitator Guide

Brown Eyes, Blue Eyes:
Linking Perceptions and Performance
Facilitator Guide

Slide 3

> ### What is Diversity?
>
> Diversity is human difference that distinguishes an individual or a group of people from others. These differences include age, appearance, culture, gender, physical ability, personal and professional style, race, sexual orientation, and other traits.
>
> ©2002 Workforce Development Group   3

Speaker Notes

"We realize that the term 'diversity' means a lot of different things to different people. In order to clarify what we are talking about here today, I want to share with you a common definition of diversity."

Review definition.

So when we talk about diversity, who are we talking about?

(Solicit 1-2 responses)

We are talking about everyone. We are talking about creating a culture that welcomes every employee and potential employee, business partner, and customer.

Facilitator Guide

Brown Eyes, Blue Eyes:
Linking Perceptions and Performance
Facilitator Guide

Slide 4

Why Does Diversity Matter?

A customer adheres to an orthodox religious practice of gender segregation in public settings.

Why might this matter in terms of how we treat her?

©2002 Workforce Development Group

4

Speaker Notes

Read slide out loud.

Solicit 2-3 participants' responses to the question.

Acknowledge participants' responses with a nod or a verbal, "Thank you." Repeat participants' responses if necessary to be sure everyone can hear. (Avoid using words like "very good" or "right!")

Note: Add your responses only if participants seem reluctant to share or are unclear about why this matters to the organization. Possible responses are provided for you on page 43 of this guide.

Facilitator Guide

Brown Eyes, Blue Eyes:
Linking Perceptions and Performance
Facilitator Guide

Slide 5

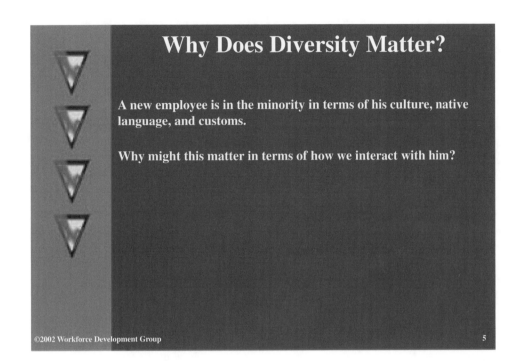

Why Does Diversity Matter?

A new employee is in the minority in terms of his culture, native language, and customs.

Why might this matter in terms of how we interact with him?

©2002 Workforce Development Group   5

Speaker Notes

Read slide out loud.

Solicit a 2-3 participants' responses to the question.

Acknowledge participants' responses with a nod or a verbal, "Thank you." Repeat participants' responses if necessary to be sure everyone can hear. (Avoid using words like "very good" or "right!")

Note: Add your responses only if participants seem reluctant to share or are unclear about why this matters to the organization. Possible responses are provided for you on page 43 of this guide.

Facilitator Guide

Brown Eyes, Blue Eyes:
Linking Perceptions and Performance
Facilitator Guide

Slide 6

Why Does Diversity Matter?

A community-based organization is committed to continuing education of under-privileged children.

Why might this matter to the organization?

©2002 Workforce Development Group   6

Speaker Notes

Read slide out loud.

Solicit a 2-3 participants' responses to the question.

Acknowledge participants' responses with a nod or a verbal, "Thank you." Repeat participants' responses if necessary to be sure everyone can hear. (Avoid using words like "very good" or "right!")

Note: Add your responses only if participants seem reluctant to share or are unclear about why this matters to the organization. Possible responses are provided for you on page 50 of this guide.

Facilitator Guide

Brown Eyes, Blue Eyes:
Linking Perceptions and Performance
Facilitator Guide

Slide 7

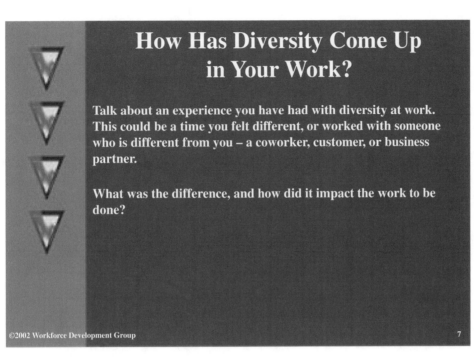

How Has Diversity Come Up in Your Work?

Talk about an experience you have had with diversity at work. This could be a time you felt different, or worked with someone who is different from you – a coworker, customer, or business partner.

What was the difference, and how did it impact the work to be done?

©2002 Workforce Development Group

7

Speaker Notes

"Let's just spend a moment talking about how diversity shows up for you at work. What I'd like you to do is pair up with someone sitting near you. Talk about an experience you have had with diversity at work. This could be a time you felt different, or worked with someone who is different from you – a coworker, customer, or member of the community. What was the difference, and how did it impact the work to be done?"

Allow participants 3-4 minutes to discuss. Solicit 2-3 participants' responses to the question. Repeat participants' responses if necessary to be sure everyone can hear. Acknowledge responses with a nod or thank participants verbally.

Summarize the conversation on why diversity is important to business, and segue into the video introduction, explaining that it will delve into what can happen if we do not actively work at promoting inclusion.

Facilitator Guide

Slide 8

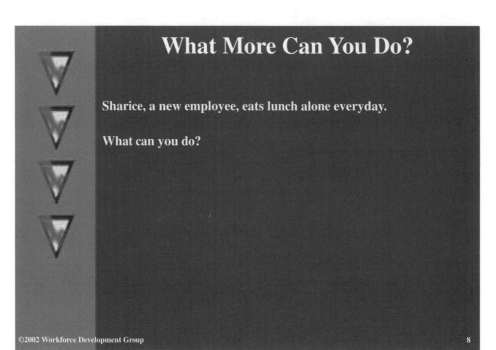

Speaker Notes

Review scenario. "This is a really common one."

Solicit 2-3 participants' responses to the question.

Repeat participants' responses if necessary to be sure everyone can hear.

Acknowledge responses with a nod or a verbal, "Thank you."

Facilitator Guide

©2002 Indra Lahiri, Ph.D.

Brown Eyes, Blue Eyes:
Linking Perceptions and Performance
Facilitator Guide

Slide 9

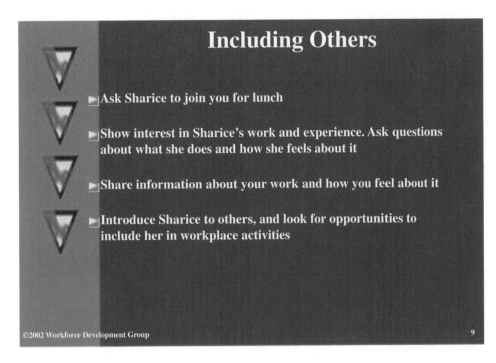

Including Others

▸ Ask Sharice to join you for lunch

▸ Show interest in Sharice's work and experience. Ask questions about what she does and how she feels about it

▸ Share information about your work and how you feel about it

▸ Introduce Sharice to others, and look for opportunities to include her in workplace activities

©2002 Workforce Development Group

9

Speaker Notes

"Here are some additional things you could do" (review and add any of your own ideas)

OR

Acknowledge the things suggested in this slide that participants also suggested, and add anything not yet covered.

Facilitator Guide

Slide 10

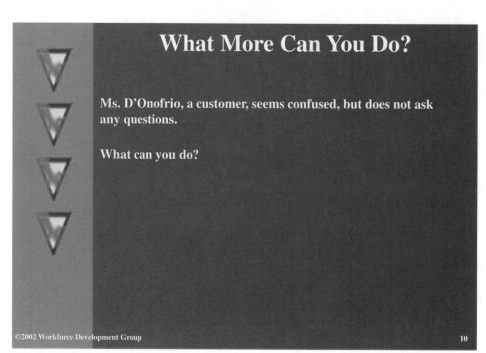

Speaker Notes

Review scenario. "Here's an important one in making sure our customers are getting the best care."

Solicit 2-3 participants' responses to the question.

Repeat participants' responses if necessary to be sure everyone can hear.

Acknowledge responses with a nod or verbal, "Thank you."

Slide 11

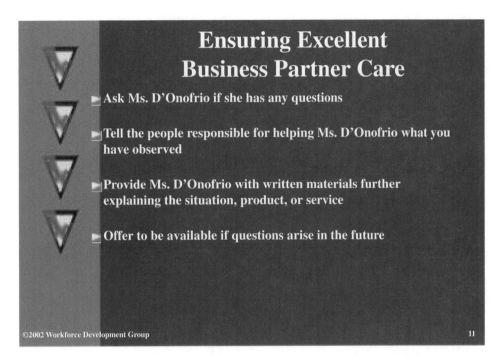

Speaker Notes

"Here are some additional things you can do." Review and add any of your own ideas.

OR

Acknowledge the things suggested in this slide that participants also suggested, and add anything not yet covered.

Facilitator Guide

Brown Eyes, Blue Eyes:
Linking Perceptions and Performance
Facilitator Guide

Slide 12

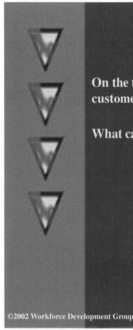

What More Can You Do?

On the telephone, you are having trouble understanding a customer who speaks English with an accent.

What can you do?

©2002 Workforce Development Group

12

Speaker Notes

Review scenario. "This is a tough one."

Solicit 2-3 participants' responses to the question.

Repeat participants' responses if necessary to be sure everyone can hear.

Acknowledge responses with a nod or verbal, "Thank you."

Facilitator Guide

Brown Eyes, Blue Eyes:
Linking Perceptions and Performance
Facilitator Guide

Slide 13

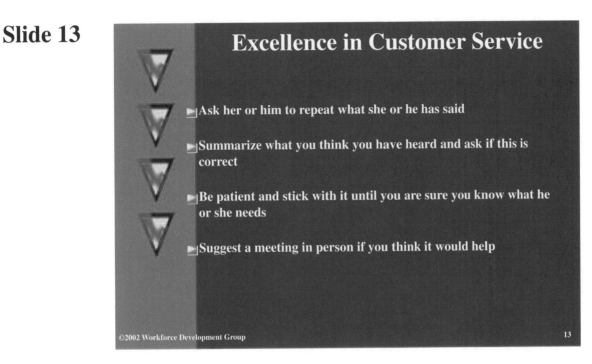

Excellence in Customer Service

▶ Ask her or him to repeat what she or he has said

▶ Summarize what you think you have heard and ask if this is correct

▶ Be patient and stick with it until you are sure you know what he or she needs

▶ Suggest a meeting in person if you think it would help

©2002 Workforce Development Group

13

Speaker Notes

"Here are some additional things you can do." Review and add any of your own ideas.

OR

Acknowledge the things suggested in this slide that participants also suggested, and add anything not yet covered.

Facilitator Guide

Brown Eyes, Blue Eyes:
Linking Perceptions and Performance
Facilitator Guide

Slide 14

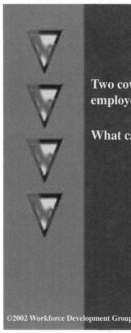

What More Can You Do?

Two coworkers are making stereotypical comments about an employee from a different ethnic background.

What can you do?

©2002 Workforce Development Group

14

Speaker Notes

Review scenario. "Well, that never happens, does it?"

Solicit 2-3 participants' responses to the question.

Repeat participants' responses if necessary to be sure everyone can hear.

Acknowledge responses with a nod or verbal, "Thank you."

Facilitator Guide

©2002 Indra Lahiri, Ph.D.

Slide 15

Creating an Inclusive Environment

▶ Remain respectful and avoid placing blame, yet help them to see that their comments are not good for anybody at work – including them

▶ Neutralize the conversation before feelings of exclusion can occur by asking, "Did I just hear what I think I heard?"

▶ Ask the coworkers what they meant by their remarks

▶ Explain the negative consequences that stereotyping and exclusion have on the business and on individuals in a manner that is not threatening but compassionate

©2002 Workforce Development Group

15

Speaker Notes

"Here are some additional things you can do." Review and add any of your own ideas.

OR

Acknowledge the things suggested in this slide that participants also suggested, and add anything not yet covered.

Facilitator Guide

Brown Eyes, Blue Eyes:
Linking Perceptions and Performance
Facilitator Guide

Slide 16

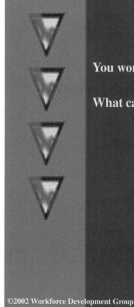

What More Can You Do?

You work in a geographic area that has very little diversity.

What can you do?

©2002 Workforce Development Group

16

Speaker Notes

Review scenario.

Solicit 2-3 participants' responses to the question.

Repeat participants' responses if necessary to be sure everyone can hear.

Acknowledge responses with a nod or verbal, "Thank you."

Slide 17

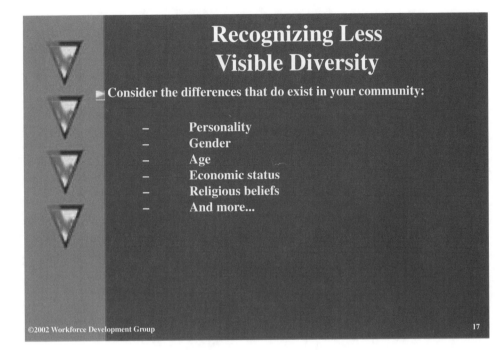

Speaker Notes

"Remember our definition of diversity. Who are we talking about? Everyone. It is easy to slip into thinking diversity is only about the differences that are easy to see— like race, gender, and age. And these are very important differences, but diversity is about much more."

"Here are some additional things you can do." Review and add any of your own ideas.

OR

Acknowledge the things suggested in this slide that participants also suggested, and add anything not yet covered.

Facilitator Guide

Slide 18

What More Can You Do?

You hear that the Diversity Council is partnering with community groups to sponsor various events.

What can you do?

©2002 Workforce Development Group   18

Speaker Notes

Review scenario.

Solicit 2-3 participants' responses to the question.

Repeat participants' responses if necessary to be sure everyone can hear.

Acknowledge responses with a nod or verbal, "Thank you."

Brown Eyes, Blue Eyes:
Linking Perceptions and Performance
Facilitator Guide

Slide 19

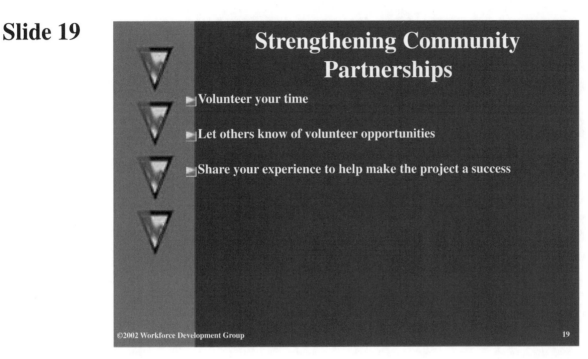

Speaker Notes

"Here are some additional things you can do." Review and add any of your own ideas.

OR

Acknowledge the things suggested in this slide that participants also suggested, and add anything not yet covered.

Facilitator Guide

Slide 20

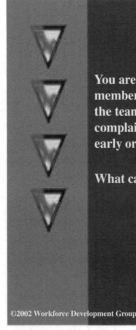

What More Can You Do?

You are the manager of a team of 6 people. Several of the team members have been grumbling that the most senior person on the team is being given special treatment. The team members complain that the senior person is often allowed to leave work early or come in late.

What can you do?

©2002 Workforce Development Group
20

Speaker Notes

"Ok, so far, we have been talking about our responsibilities as individual contributors. Here's one for managers."

Review scenario.

Solicit 2-3 responses from people with management responsibilities, then take 1-2 suggestions from non-managers.

Repeat participants' responses if necessary to be sure everyone can hear.

Acknowledge responses with a nod or verbal, "Thank you."

Facilitator Guide

Slide 21

Building an Inclusive Team

► Give your employees an opportunity to address their concerns honestly, openly, and respectfully instead of grumbling

► If employees have specific work / life balance needs, talk these through and determine whether there is a way that you can support them, and get the work done

► Identify any additional issues that may be affecting team work and ask employees for their suggestions on how to improve the situation

©2002 Workforce Development Group

21

Speaker Notes

"Here are some additional things you can do." Review and add any of your own ideas.

OR

Acknowledge the things suggested in this slide that participants also suggested, and add anything not yet covered.

Slide 22

> ## What More Can You Do?
>
> You have just hired a person of a different racial background than any other members of your team. You want to set this person up for equal success as other team members, and recognize that there will be challenges, many of them very subtle, to overcome.
>
> What can you do?
>
> ©2002 Workforce Development Group   22

Speaker Notes

"Here's another one for managers."

Review scenario.

Solicit 2-3 responses from people with management responsibilities, then take 1-2 suggestions from non-managers.

Repeat participants' responses if necessary to be sure everyone can hear.

Acknowledge responses with a nod or verbal, "Thank you."

Facilitator Guide

Brown Eyes, Blue Eyes:
Linking Perceptions and Performance
Facilitator Guide

Slide 23

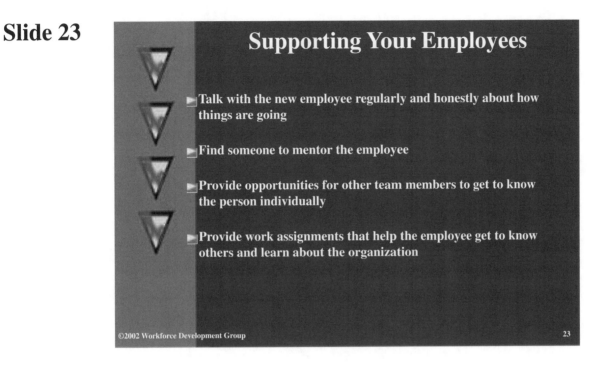

Speaker Notes

"Here are some additional things you can do." Review and add any of your own ideas.

OR

Acknowledge the things suggested in this slide that participants also suggested, and add anything not yet covered.

Brown Eyes, Blue Eyes:
Linking Perceptions and Performance
Facilitator Guide

Slide 24

Action Learning Assignment

▶ Clearly state some deliberate actions you will take to apply today's learning with coworkers and/or customers.

▶ Identify how you will report on your progress—what is going differently as a result of your actions.

▶ State some learning objectives—things you would like to learn to do better as you work with others.

©2002 Workforce Development Group

24

Speaker Notes

"So here is what I'd like each one of you to do between now and (date). Consider the list we came up with of things we can do to address the dynamics we saw in the film. Come up with target actions that you can focus on immediately to make a difference. The three components of your action learning assignment are right here on this slide."

(Explain points from the slide using your own words to elaborate as needed.)

Facilitator Guide

Brown Eyes, Blue Eyes:
Linking Perceptions and Performance
Facilitator Guide

Slide 25

> ## Action Learning Assignment:
> ## Sample Types of Activities
>
> ▶ Seek out and use ideas, opinions, and insights from diverse and various sources
>
> ▶ Maximize effectiveness by using individuals' particular talents and abilities on tasks or assignments
>
> ▶ Recruit and/or develop individuals from various backgrounds and cultures
>
> ©2002 Workforce Development Group   25

Speaker Notes

"The kinds of activities you can consider for your action learning assignment may vary. The next few slides offer many examples of types of activities, though of course you will need to be more specific in creating your own action learning assignment."

Review slide in your own words.

Facilitator Guide

Slide 26

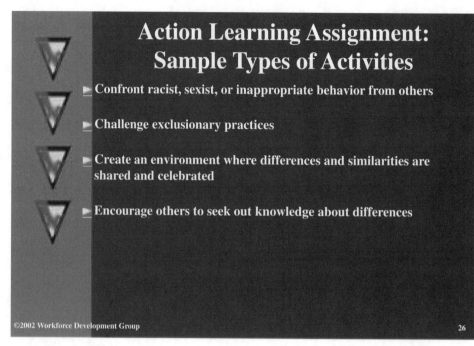

Action Learning Assignment:
Sample Types of Activities

▶ Confront racist, sexist, or inappropriate behavior from others

▶ Challenge exclusionary practices

▶ Create an environment where differences and similarities are shared and celebrated

▶ Encourage others to seek out knowledge about differences

©2002 Workforce Development Group   26

Speaker Notes

Review slide in your own words.

Slide 27

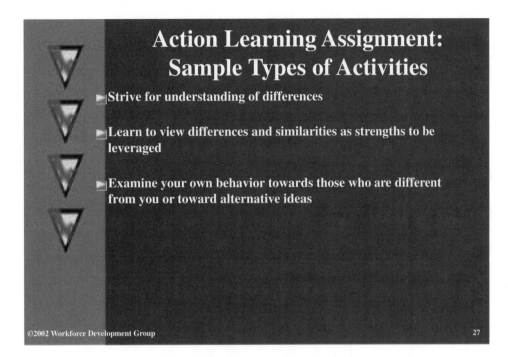

Action Learning Assignment:
Sample Types of Activities

▶ Strive for understanding of differences

▶ Learn to view differences and similarities as strengths to be leveraged

▶ Examine your own behavior towards those who are different from you or toward alternative ideas

©2002 Workforce Development Group   27

Speaker Notes

Review slide in your own words.